magic
METAL

Buildings of Steel, Aluminium, Copper and Tin

Imprint
The Deutsche Bibliothek is registering this publication in the
Deutsche Nationalbibliographie; detailed bibliographical infor-
mation can be found on the internet at http://dnb.ddb.de

ISBN 978-3-938780-31-2

© 2008 by Verlagshaus Braun
www.verlagshaus-braun.de

1st edition 2008

Editorial staff:
Anna Hinc, Jacob Hochrein, Susanne Laßwitz, Sophie Steybe
Translation:
Stephen Roche, Hamburg
Graphic concept and layout:
Michaela Prinz
Reproduction:
LVD Gesellschaft für Datenverarbeitung mbH, Berlin

magic
METAL

Buildings of Steel, Aluminium, Copper and Tin

Projects selected by
Dirk Meyhöfer

BRAUN

Magic metal

It's no exaggeration, more an accurate observation, to say that the glittering union of glass and steel has become the salient feature of late-twentieth-century architecture. What this represents is not just the rise of steel but of metal in general as the key material in modern architecture. Metal is 'hot'.

There is a curious aspect to metal's advance. It was the triumph of iron as the building material par excellence of the 19th century that opened up new and hitherto unprecedented freedom in the construction of bridges, monumental halls and railway stations. This development found its sequel in the age of steel, a building material which – combined with concrete – forms the backbone of modern construction technology. Then, however, two principles that already dominated modern art began to gain acceptance in architecture: reduction and abstraction. Mies van der Rohe's motto, less is more, was initially applied only to matters of style. Eventually, though – thanks to technological progress – engineers also caught the bug. Dreams of delicacy and transparency led to an absolutist minimalism: load-bearing steel columns and beams suddenly had to be hidden from view. The invention of structural glazing at the same time as high performance glass such as LSG promised to make this dream a reality: enormous glass panes could now be supported by slender steel plates.

Metal's advance was further aided by the development of computers. Their immense efficiency as tools finally gave engineers and architects the freedom to cast off the millennia-old philosophy of tectonics. Instead of beams and supports, we now have skin and bones, daring systems of membranes in exceptionally elegant and dynamic forms. Does this herald the end of steel's leading role? Far from it. The era of metals and alloys has only just begun.

This book deals not only with iron, but with all metals that play a role in construction, many of which have been in use for centuries. Copper and zinc, for example, are classic materials in the construction of churches and cathedrals; as such they represent a venerable tradition of craftsmanship. Few materials retain their technical function and effectiveness as design elements as well as zinc and copper. The latter forms its own protective layer, its characteristic green patina that only reaches full bloom with age.

Quality, durability and beauty are attributes that have made copper and its alloys popular for centuries. Now, at the dawn of the 21st century its combination of sustainability and aesthetics is once again in great demand. In addition, technology now makes it possible to speed up the ageing process, thus further improving the surface features. How and whether one uses copper is a question of belief, some would say faith. In any case, its design possibilities have grown.

Zinc plate is an equally old material. It is used today almost exclusively in the form of titanium zinc. It lasts for up to 100 years and requires neither maintenance nor repair, provided it was correctly manufactured in the first place. Zinc plate is sold in the form of coils or sheets. For roof cladding metal tracks (courses) are used. Mostly these are only 60 centimetres in width but up to 10 metres in length. Modern architecture is coming up with ever more extravagant applications for zinc plate. One of the best recent examples is Daniel Libeskind's Jewish Museum in Berlin.

When aluminium was first discovered in the 19th century it was as rare and precious as gold. The basic characteristics of this modern building material – its negligible weight, its strength, elasticity and resistance to corrosion – inspired some of the 20th century's greatest artists, designers and engineers, such as Frank Lloyd Wright, Buckminster Fuller and Philippe Stark. Architects approach this material from a variety of angles and tend to show equal interest in its technological development as in its aesthetic value in architecture and industrial design.

Metal has an almost unlimited number of potential applications in architecture. Beyond structurally determined uses, we can approximately narrow these down to core applications.

The first is a direct result of metal's structural properties; we are talking here about its use as the skeleton, the 'bones' of a building. These have tended to be less frequently disguised in recent times, fire protection measures permitting. In the past massive skeletal structures were used to create colossal machines for the coal mining industry, for iron- and steelworks and in chemical engineering. In most cases these structures were developed incidentally, but always guided by their function. In the 1970s Renzo Piano built a monument to this type of early industrial architecture with the Pompidou Centre in Paris. Among contemporary work the award-winning Schwarzbergschanze project in Klingenthal (m2r-architecture, London, page 42) takes up a similar challenge: On the one hand the tower and ski-jump represent a decidedly ambitious structure. Precisely because of its challenging use of materials it became known as a 'lighthouse' project. The ski-jump takes advantage of an essential characteristic of metal: it can be supplied in prefabricated form (either as individual parts or modules) and assembled on site.

A complex building such as a ski jump, by incorporating a swinging ramp and a capsule at its summit, becomes a highly modern example of architettura parlante!

The second of metal's three core applications may appear two-dimensional at first glance yet governs the very essence of a building: its façade! This can also be understood as a skin – our third skin – if it is built, as it often is these days, as an intelligent façade system that combines wall and façade in one.

While a façade doesn't have to have the near-literary sophistication of, say Francis Soler's Ministry of Culture in Paris it does, nevertheless, produce effects and affects that are independent of the materials used. Moreover, it produces useful applications in terms of that key function of a building – to provide shelter. Metals are tough materials, and most of them rust or – like copper – change their skin. Metals age gracefully, and unlike newer synthetic materials they do not decay. On the contrary, and most relevantly in light of our recent embrace of sustainability, metals can be scrapped, and therefore recycled.

The use of metals in architectural façades is reminiscent of haute couture. While it is rare enough that an architect is inspired directly by a fashion designer – as Jan Kaplicky was by Gaultier when he designed Selfridge's department store in Birmingham – often the punched plates or sidings are put together as ingeniously and elaborately as a piece of designer clothing. Almost every example included in this book contains the stuff that architects' dreams are made of. Computer programs help in punching, and technology constantly invents new methods of colouring metals or helping them to achieve their predestined patina.

The third major application of metal is sculptural: Metal is flexible enough to encase any building regardless of its form. Space and body are the 'free leg', the basis of all architecture. Metal then is the material that makes this possible – no wonder it has maintained its popularity over the centuries. Sculpture needs a skin, skin needs bones – the circle is complete. Truly magical metal!

Dirk Meyhöfer

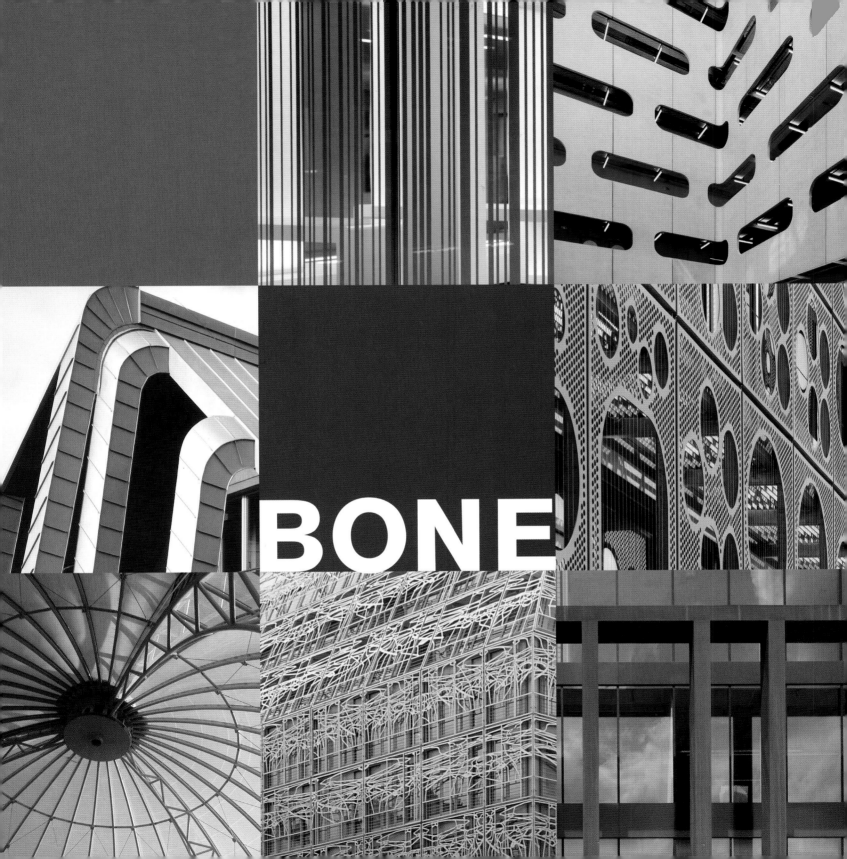

BONE

New City Centre Vaihingen, 2004
Address: Hauptstraße, Vaihinger Markt, Stuttgart,
Germany. **Client:** Senator h.c. Rudi Häussler, Stuttgart.
Gross floor area: 103,000 m².

Five façades
ARCHITECTS:
Léon Wohlhage Wernik Architekten, Berlin

The departure of a huge brewery vacated a town-cen-
tre site and offered the chance to finally give the town
of Vaihingen a true urban centre. Thus the Schwaben-
galerie shopping complex was born – a section of urban
space with public buildings and squares. The tender
invitation called for an American-style shopping mall,
an introspective climate-controlled world. What have
emerged are European-style urban spaces, public
spaces with squares and lanes that knit the new quarter
to the larger urban fabric of this medieval town in the
Stuttgart commuter belt. Thus the old town hall square
has been "moved" from the periphery to the centre of
the town and three new pedestrian precincts now lead
to another square, elevated seven metres higher. The
new Civic Forum and the market hall are situated between the squares. Other structures are arranged in
the form of three urban blocks with shops, offices and
DaimlerChrysler's Mo-Hotel. The centrepiece of the ensemble is the so-called Atrium, a glass hall with a double
function: as the winter counterpart to the open square,
the two forming a unit; and as the skylight for, and path
to and from, the underground car park.

04

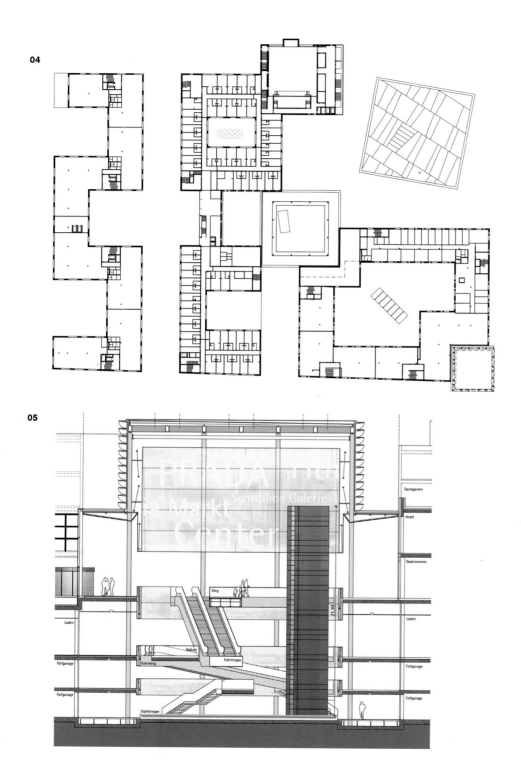

01 Main view **02** Interior view **03** Exterior view **04** Building blocks **05** Atrium vertical section **06** View from the gallery

05

Duchgarten

Hotel

Gastronomie

Laden

Laden

Steg

Tiefgarage

Balkon

Fahrtreppe

Fahrsteig

Tiefgarage

Stahltreppe

Tiefgarage

Orang-utan house in the Hagenbeck Zoo, 2004
Address: Tierpark Hagenbeck, Lokstedter Grenz-
straße 2, 22527 Hamburg, Germany. **Client:** Hagenbeck
Gemeinnützige Gesellschaft mbH, Hamburg. **Gross
floor area:** 1,100 m². **Materials:** steel-ribbed dome
infilled with ETFE film cushions.

A house for primates
ARCHITECTS: PSP Architekten Ingenieure,
Hamburg

The orang-utan house in Hamburg's Hagenbeck Zoo
is a "covered outdoor enclosure." A steel-framed dome
approximately 32 meters in diameter ascends into the
Hamburg sky above a supporting base structure of reinforced concrete. Stalls, equipment rooms and adjoining
service areas are located within the foundation of the
dome's supporting structure. The dome accommodates
mainly the spacious animal enclosure and visitor area. It
was designed with the aim of simulating the climate of
the orang-utans' native Sumatran habitat. This has been
successfully achieved under the insulated, ribbed dome
with its infilling of multilayered, air-filled membrane
cushions between the steel profiles. A motor-driven
mechanism opens the roof halfway. The ETFE film used
is highly pervious to ultraviolet radiation and so helps to
create an environment congenial to both man and ape
by allowing the plants inside to thrive.

01 View into the dome **02** Floor plan **03** Exterior view with opened
dome

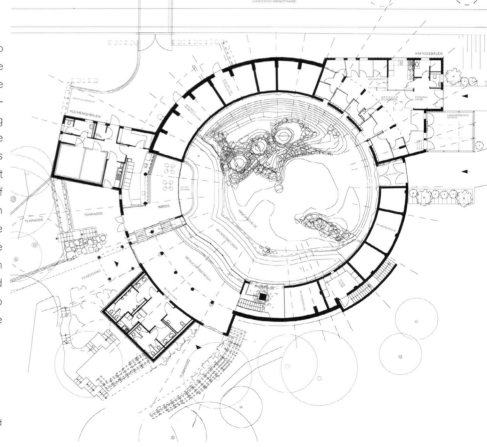

02

Hohen Luckow residential house, 2001
Address: Hohen Luckow estate, Rostocker
Straße 23, 18239 Hohen Luckow, Germany. **Client:**
Hohen Luckow estate. **Structural design:** Ingenieur-
büro Hasenberg, Lichtenhagen. **Gross floor area:**
300 m². **Roof material:** preweathered titanium zinc.

Back to the future

ARCHITECTS: she_architekten and
Anna B. Nicolas, Hamburg

This project represents a successful attempt to apply
lateral thinking within traditional parameters. Situated
next to the restored outbuildings of the historical Hohen Luckow estate, this building conforms with its form,
eaves height and roof pitch to the traditional North German thatched "longhouse", a timber-framed farm building that contained living quarters, a stable area and
harvest storage under one roof. The architects have
produced a modern take on this traditional design, drop-
ping the gable roof right down to ground level at the
narrow ends of the house. With a sharp kink in the ridge,
the titanium-clad roof folds over the entrance façade at
one end and stretches protectively to the ground with
tentacle-like arms at the other.

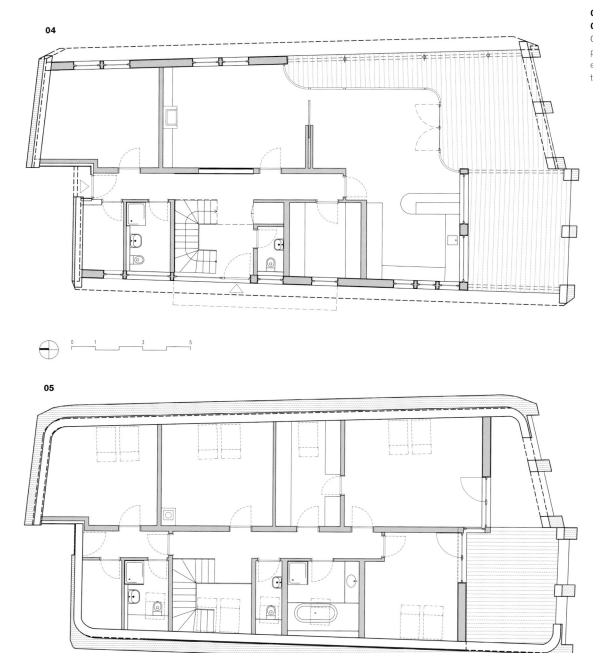

04

05

0 1   3   5

0 1   3   5

01 Garden side from north east
02 Living space with terrace 03
Opening to south 04 Ground floor
plan 05 Upper floor plan 06 Northern side with side entrance, view
through the house axis

18

"Les Bons Enfants", 2005
Remodelling of the Central Services Building of the Ministry of Culture and Communication
Address: Rue St. Honoré, Paris 1, France. **Client:** Ministry of Culture and Communication. **Gross floor area:** 30,000 m².

Smoothing the façades
ARCHITECTS:
Francis Soler with Frédéric Druot (interior design) and Michel Desvigne (garden)

A stone's throw from Rue de Valois, where in 1959 André Malraux created the Ministry of Culture, the different departments responsible for administration, for architecture and heritage, international development, books, reading and the archives, have gone about their business in better living and working conditions than before. Taking the view that it was essential and urgent to re-establish coherence by skilfully and sensitively reintegrating the site into Paris, Francis Soler pursued the idea that beyond all these recent archaeological layers, only by local demolitions, by rethickening the buildings, by smoothing the façades and by a general rewriting, could the whole be made accessible to an homogeneous reading, a single ministry. All the light that penetrates into the buildings is fractured and patterned by the latticework on the façade. Light is the raw material of its architecture and its interiors, and the surrounding latticework transmits all the grey skies of Paris down to the pavement.

01 Metal "hairnet" detail 02 Front
corner 03 Garden 04 Reception
hall 05 Corridor 06 Ground floor
plan 07 Section

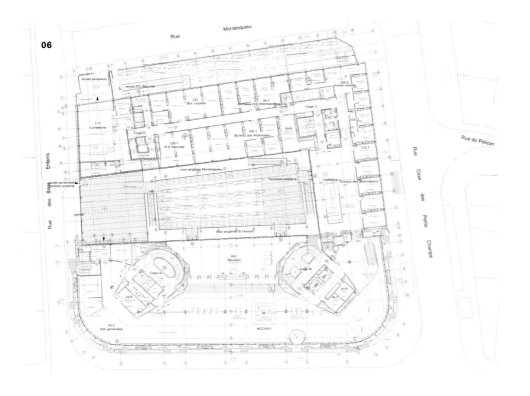

06

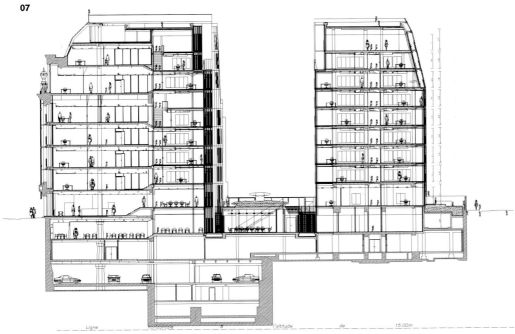

07

Total Service Stations, Hellebecq, 2002
Address: Hellebecq Area, Brussels-Tournai A8, Belgium. **Client:** TotalFinaElf Belgium S.A. **Gross floor area:** 7,875 m². **Materials:** galvanised steel, concrete, wood, glass.

Along the highway
ARCHITECTS / ENGINEERS:
Philippe SAMYN and PARTNERS

A large awning in sheet metal sections, floating on the site like a greenhouse in an agricultural landscape, covers the stations, the service centres and the restaurant area. It lends a sense of coherence to the ensemble. Its steel framework acts as a wide-mesh trellis through which natural light abundantly irrigates the various service areas. Taking advantage of the existing relief, the construction of the restaurant-bridge enables limitation of the footprint of the buildings at ground level and enhances the landscaping of the site itself. The bridge spans the highway without a central pillar. Its narrow and elongated shape allows motorists taking a short rest stop to enjoy from each table a panoramic view of the open landscape on both sides. Large galvanized expanded metal screens are fitted outside the façades of the restaurant and on the sides of the service stations. Together with the landscaping of the site, these provide visual and climatic comfort to users.

01 Site plan **02 + 03** Exterior view

**Südwestmetall Heilbronn new branch offices, 2004
Address:** Südwestmetall Heilbronn, Ferdinand-Braun-Str. 18, 74074 Heilbronn, Germany. **Client:** Südwest-metall Stuttgart. **Gross floor area:** 1,262 m². **Materials:** reinforced concrete, glass, stainless steel, sisal carpeting, Corian (mineral/polymer composite), two-component epoxy resin coating.

Transparency, reflection and flowing space
ARCHITECTS: Dominik Dreiner Architekt

This glass building for Südwestmetall, the metal industry federation for the state of Baden-Württemberg, stands on a raised foundation in open landscape. The thin glass membrane produces the effect that one barely notices the transition from interior to exterior space. The 76-metre-long and 18.5-metre-wide building is located at the edge of a park. It's form is clear and reduced; a stern rectangular block, framed by a wide, raised foundation and overhanging roof. Like a half-tone photographic print, a blow-up, the metallic surfaces reflect their surroundings, producing a shimmering image. In dull weather conditions the building seems to melt into its surroundings, whereas on bright summer days its contours are clearly defined. The metal weave consists of just 0.4 mm-thick and 50-mm wide stainless steel ribbons that are "woven" into a "warp and weft" metal braid using a specially developed "loom".

04

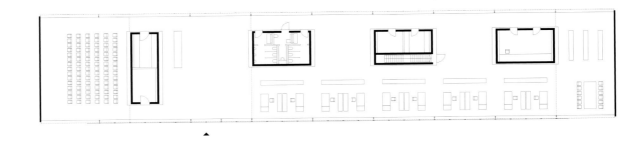

05

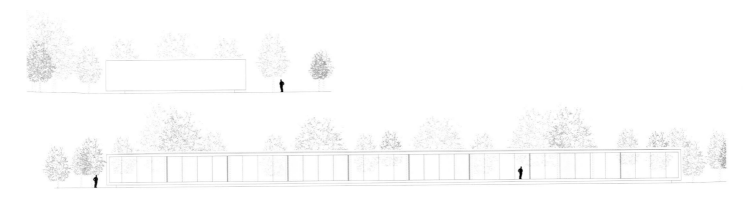

06

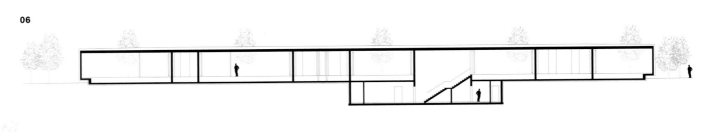

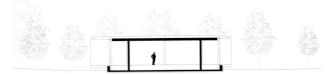

LBK Infothek, Munich, 2006
Address: Blumenstraße 19, 80331 Munich, Germany.
Client: Stadtwerke München GmbH. **Gross floor area:**
2,200 m². **Materials:** Cladding: anodized aluminium,
stainless steel; Substructure: galvanized steel.

Glass appendix

ARCHITECTS: **ssk**projektgemeinschaft
Straub – Schneider – Kern
Dipl.-Ing. Architekten München
Ver.de Landschaftsarchitektur Freising

This building was completely renovated, extended and
converted for use by the Urban Building Inspection Authority of the city of Munich (LBK: Lokalbaukommis-
sion). The designers came up with a kind of architectural aperçu: a glazed extension for the authority's service
centre. The main body of the extension is clad with anodized aluminium. The colour and depth of the material
engages with the brick cladding of the old building; the
joints fade into the background thanks to the brightness
and colour of the material. Undivided glazing, running
around three sides and framed by a stainless steel edg-
ing, juts out from the base structure. It was possible to
minimise the size of the frame by using steel furring.
The result is an extensive display window.

04

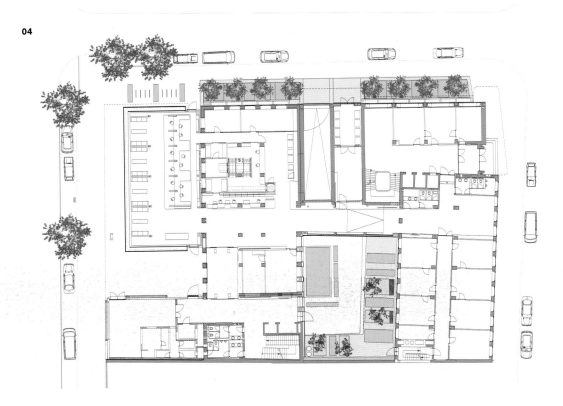

05

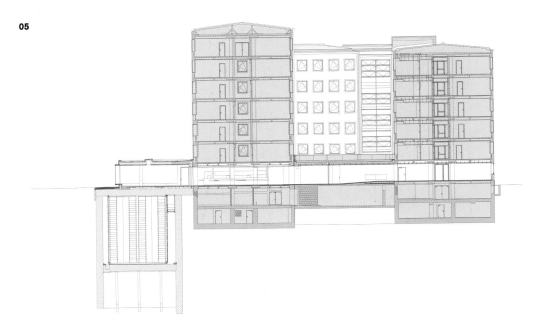

Jussieu university building, 2006
Address: Jussieu University, 10 rue Cuvier, 75005 Paris, France. **Client:** Établissement Public du Campus de Jussieu (EPCJ). **Gross floor area:** 16,895 m².

Vertical space

ARCHITECTS: Périphériques architects – Emmanuelle Marin, Anne-Françoise Jumeau and David Trottin

The 16M building on the Jussieu university campus, near the historic centre of Paris, extends and completes the grid plan that architect Edouard Albert designed in the 1960s to serve 45,000 students and researchers. The response formulated by Périphériques for the extension is based on the existing system, where buildings are laid out in a crown configuration. However, at the same the new building deforms the existing system: where Albert laid out a single patio, Périphériques have planned two. One of them is covered by bridge-buildings raised on pilotis to create short-cuts in the ring-like circulation route, and forms a "vertical space" that concentrates all movement within the building. The heaviness and hardness of this concrete space contrasts with the light-weight metal cladding of the outer skin. The façades are glazed in the same pattern as Albert's existing building. But the glass metal skin – which is composed of ten types of panels perforated with circular holes of different sizes – gives the façades complex and variable depth. The holes also filter daylight and reflections over the glass surface, thereby creating shimmering effects that give the building a constantly changing appearance, and reminding us that the original plan has "shifted".

01 Main view **02** Façade detail **03**
Interior view **04** View from the gallery **05** Entrance area **06** View to
the roof **07** Floor plan **08** Section

07

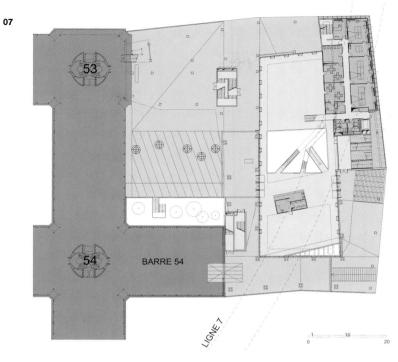

BARRE 54

LIGNE 7

08

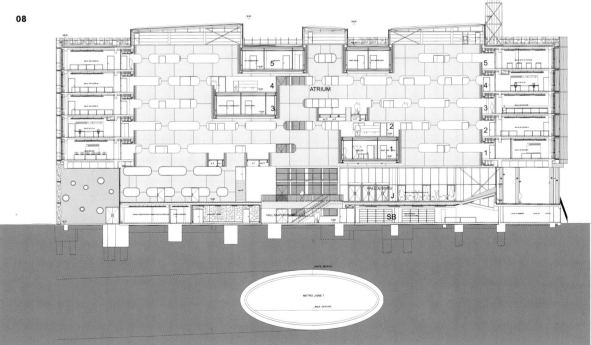

Kiel Central Railway Station, 2006
Address: Sophienblatt, 24114 Kiel, Germany. **Client:**
Deutsche Bahn AG. **Gross floor area:** 6,600 m². **Mate-**
rials: glass, steel, anodized aluminium.

New meets old

ARCHITECTS: Gössler Kreienbaum Architekten
Bernhard Gössler Martin Kreienbaum,
Hamburg & Berlin

The architects' original commission was to renovate this
station building. During the planning stage however it
emerged that the structure was skewed, due to dis-
placement in the building land towards the Kiel fjord,
making it impossible to determine the load-bearing
capacity. For this reason only the concourse could be
renovated, while the hall covering the platforms had to
be demolished and replaced by a new structure. Its roof
sheeting is fitted with almond-shaped skylights that
provide natural lighting for the building. The underside
of the roof is clad with bright, perforated metal panels
that reflect light while absorbing sound, thus providing
a pleasant environment in which to wait for one's train
connection.

03

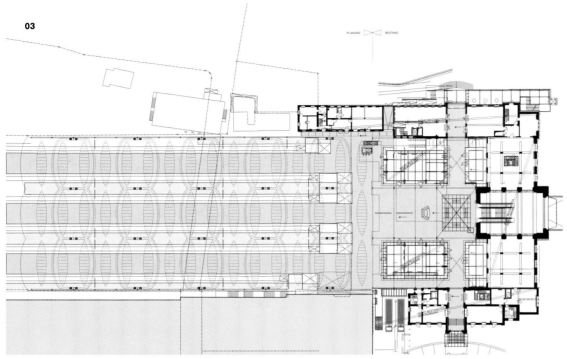

PLANUNG ⋈ BESTAND

04

PLANUNG ⋈ BESTAND

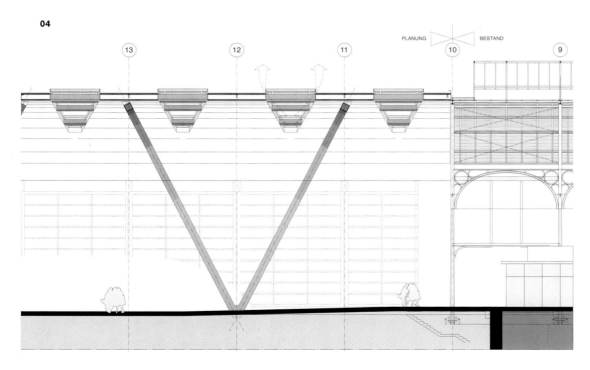

⑬ ⑫ ⑪ ⑩ ⑨

01

Ski Jump Vogtland Arena, 2005
Address: Klingenthal, Vogtland, Germany. **Client:** Vogtlandkreis District Administration. **Materials:** zinc-coated steel, aluminium cladding, glass, concrete.

Landmark in the mountains
ARCHITECTS: m2r-architecture, London

The new Vogtland Arena in Klingenthal is a regeneration project that hopes to bring life and jobs back to an area that was once one of the finest ski resorts in former East Germany. The invention of lightweight materials has led to radical improvements in skiing equipment and has changed the sport significantly. This project sought to reflect and incorporate similar advances in both technology and vision in the ski jump. The result is a steel structure that is as light as possible and expresses the elegance and precision of this sport. Due to the difficulties involved in accessing the construction site a high level of prefabrication was required. Only thus was it possible to achieve high quality while meeting the programme's tight schedule. The new structure was developed in single components that could be modified later to attain optimal performance. The entire on-site construction period was a mere four months. The 35-metre-high capsule is an imaginative light source that appears to float above the treetops. It is a beacon visible from afar and has become an eye-catching landmark in the mountains.

02

04

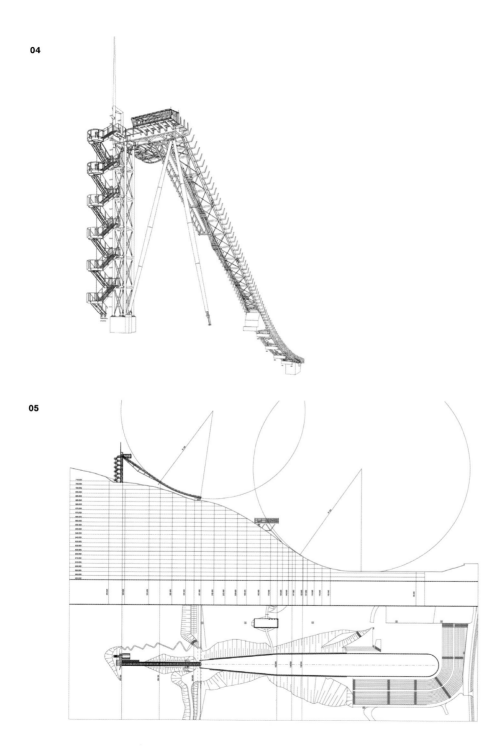

05

Light rail station, The Hague, 2006
Address: Beatrixlaan, The Hague, The Netherlands.
Client: Municipality of The Hague. **Project organisation:** RandstadRail. **Materials:** steel / stainless steel, glass, concrete.

Ringed skeleton structure
ARCHITECTS: Zwarts & Jansma Architects

RandstadRail is a project to create a new light rail network for the area between The Hague and Rotterdam. The 400-metre-long viaduct by Zwarts & Jansma comprises a ringed skeleton of mild steel bands with a circumference of about 10 metres, interconnected by hollow, diagonally arranged bars to form an open tube structure. The considerable structural height of the tube allows it to easily cover the large spans. The structure is supported by V-shaped columns and provides room for two rail tracks, allowing two trains to pass within the tube. Thanks to the massive spans of 40 and 50 metres there are relatively few columns at street level. There is also hardly any visual obstruction at eye level, so that pedestrian and traffic safety are not compromised. The new Beatrixlaan station encompasses a platform in the middle of the tube with the railway tracks diverging around a central platform. The spatial form of the station derives from a combination of the alignment and the profile of empty space. This means that the station building is precisely long enough for the trains to travel around the platform in an ideal curve.

01 Escalators **02** Tube section **03** In the tube, view to the south **04** Exterior view

02

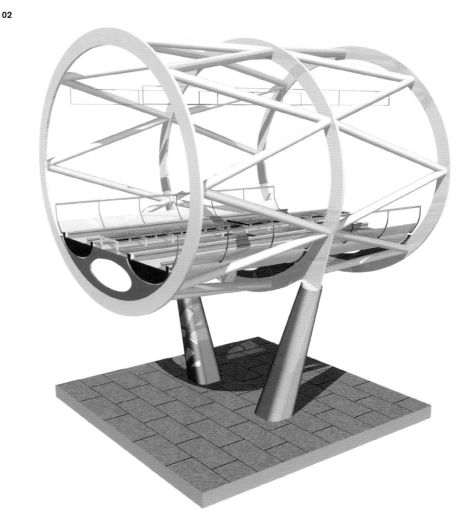

THS Administrative Building, Nordstern Colliery, 2003
Address: Nordsternplatz 1, 45899 Gelsenkirchen, Germany. **Client:** TreuHandStelle GmbH, Essen. **Gross floor area:** 17,100 m². **Materials:** main load-bearing structure: steel-binding structure; façade: suspended steel framework with filler wall of clinker brick; other materials: concrete, plastered masonry, glass, wood, poured asphalt.

Fritz Schupp reloaded
ARCHITECTS: Architektenteam THS / PASD
Feldmeier _ Wrede

When converting the Nordstern colliery into an administrative building it was important that the original building complex designed by Fritz Schupp was retained as far as possible. Following closely the intention of Schupp's design, which strives to achieve convertibility and adaptability in industrial buildings, the steel lattice framework structure was adapted to the new requirements. The old, mostly enclosed, wall structure of the façade had to be opened by means of window bands in order to facilitate the projected work spaces. At the heart of the complex is the "reading hall", located in the former warehouse, which was converted into the central hall after being completely gutted. It was a challenge to insert staircases, transparent lifts and toilet blocks in order to create a space for exhibitions and cultural events.

01

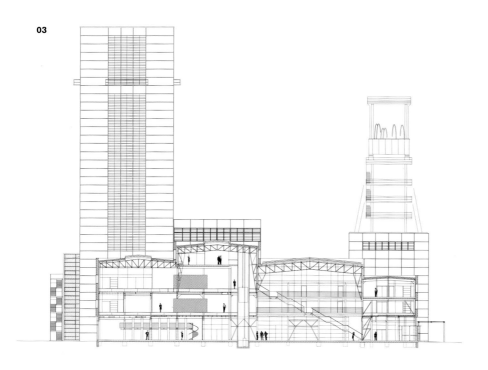

01 Internal view of hall, view towards shaft | **02** Internal view of hall **03** Section **04** Ground floor **05** Second upper floor **06** Conference room, second floor **07** Corridor, third floor

04

05

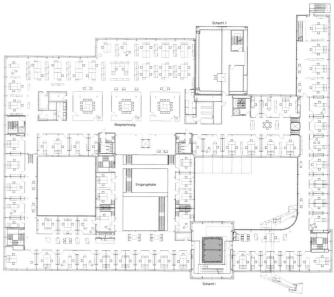

01

Forum Messe – Trade fair centre
Event venues, exhibition spaces, cafeteria and conference rooms
Address: Ludwig-Erhard-Anlage 1, 60327 Frankfurt am Main, Germany. **Interior design:** Index Architekten. **Lighting design:** ag Licht. **Client:** Messe Frankfurt GmbH. **Gross floor area:** 22,750 m². **Materials:** reinforced concrete structure, aluminium-clad outer shell (exterior); Bitu-Terrazzo surfacing, oak industrial parquet, slit acoustic panels in Canadian maple (interior).

Sweeping form
ARCHITECTS: KSP Engel und Zimmermann Architekten, Frankfurt

A sweeping metal form marks the entrance to the Frankfurt trade fair complex. Together with the Agora, the Forum marks the heart of the trade fair grounds, its light structure and transparent façades contrasting with the solid mass of the Festhalle behind it. Clear, column-free spaces on both of the main levels allow for the kind of structural versatility that is needed to accommodate any event from conferences to banquets, from trade fairs to exhibitions. The shell of the building plays dramatically with light and space. By day, the hustle and bustle of the fair is reflected in the expanses of glass. In the evening and at night, the spatial and visual boundaries dissolve. The transition from interior to exterior is barely perceptible.

02

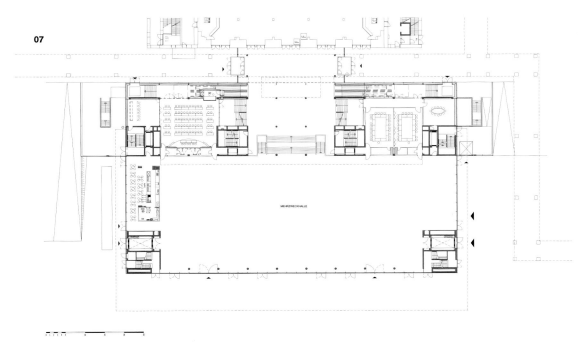

01 A sweeping curved form marks the prelude to the exhibition area of the trade fair **02** The metal bracket of the banquet hall appears to hang suspended above the Agora **03** Forum building **04** Apex of the bracket, also entrance to the banquet hall **05** Mezzanine floor, cafeteria **06** View into the exhibition and trade fair area on the ground floor **07** Ground floor plan **08** Section

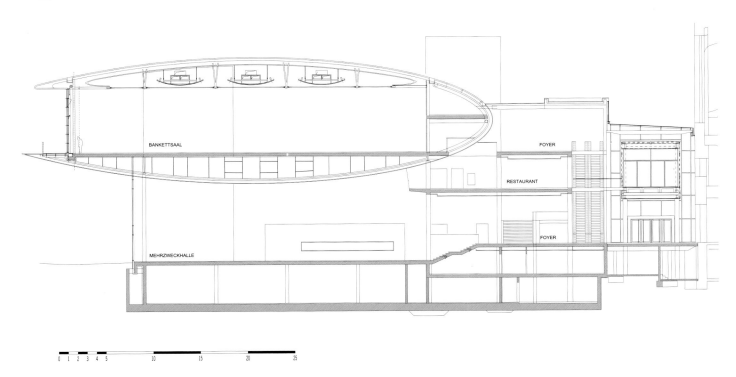

0 1 2 3 4 5   10   15   20   25

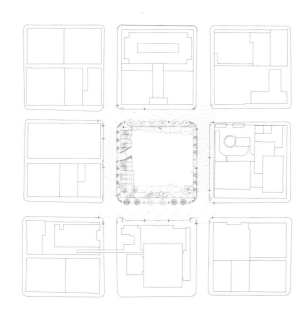

Seattle Central Library, 2004
Engineer: Arup / Magnusson Klemencic Associates.
Client: Seattle Public Library. **Gross floor area:**
38,300 m² library, including 33,700 m² of offices,
reading room, book spiral, mixing chamber, meeting
platform, living room, staff floor, children's collection
and auditorium, and 4,600 m² of parking.

Spiral of books
ARCHITECTS: OMA | LMN joint venture

OMA's ambition is to redefine the library as an institution no longer exclusively dedicated to the book, but rather as an information storehouse where all potent forms of media — new and old — are presented equally and accessibly. In an age where information can be accessed anywhere, it is the simultaneity of all media and (more importantly) the curatorship of their contents that will make the library vital. An important section of the building is the "Books Spiral", (designed to display the library's non-fiction collection without breaking up the Dewey Decimal classification system into different floors or sections). The collection spirals up through four storeys on a continuous series of shelves. This allows patrons to peruse the entire collection without using stairs or travelling to a different part of the building. Typical of OMA's design is the varied use of lighting and colour as an orientation aid, both in daylight and at night.

01 Site plan **02** View from the corner of 4th and Madison Street **03** 5th Avenue entrance

Tivoli Concert Hall, 2005
New practising facility, lounge and conference centre
Address: Vesterbrogade 3, Copenhagen, Denmark.
Client: Tivoli. **Gross floor area:** 4,000 m². **Materials:**
white lacquered, twisted aluminium strips.

The spirit of the Tivoli
ARCHITECTS: 3XN Architects, Copenhagen

In 2004, 3XN was given the prestigious task of reno-
vating and extending the concert hall in the Tivoli Gardens, Copenhagen's long-famous amusement park. The
venerable hall has been renovated in keeping with its
historical surroundings; the building has been gently
modernized and improved in order to meet the modern requirements of a concert hall. A new extension has
been realized in a light, transparent design that comple-
ments the existing Tivoli pavilion architecture. The so-
called Rainbow Hall in the basement under the concert
hall has been changed into a cloakroom with a lobby
area and restrooms, and has – as its most spectacular
feature – a beautiful 30-metre-long shark tank covering one wall of the lobby. The new pavilion should match
Tivoli's playful ambience. Twisted aluminium strips with
white lacquer provide the right "harlequin" pattern, with
a modern, yet playful, look and feel.

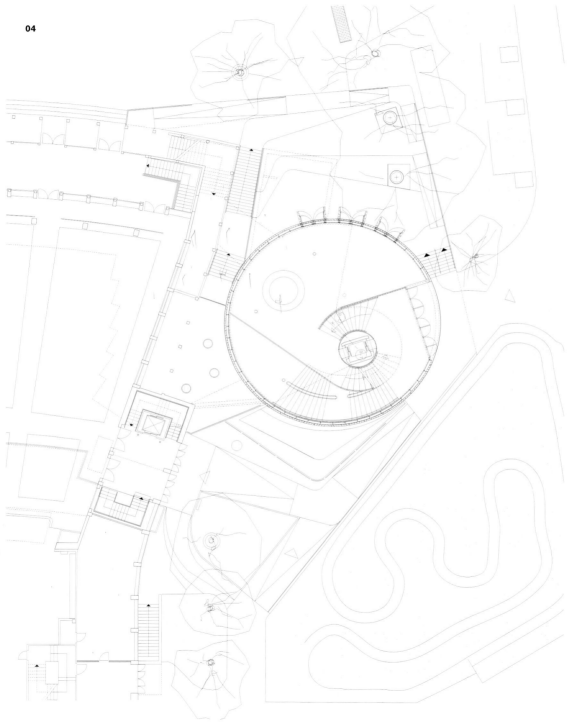

04

01 Street façade 02 New pavilion
03 Twisted aluminium strips blend
in well with the old concert hall
building's decorations 04 Ground
floor 05 Twisted aluminium strips
allow for great transparency

SKIN

Kai 13, 2004
Office and commercial building
Address: Kaistraße 13, 40221 Düsseldorf, Germany.
Client: Engel Canessa Projektentwicklung, Pension
Fund of the Chamber of Architects of the State of
North Rhine-Westphalia. **Gross floor area:** 9,100 m².
Materials: copper, TECU patina.

A precise sense of order
ARCHITECTS:
Döring Dahmen Joeressen Architekten

With its clear and rigorous architecture, this building
provides something that is in short supply in this open-
air architectural showroom on the Rhine: visual tranquillity. This is achieved through conscious restraint favour-
ing the right angle. The continuous copper skin plays a
crucial role. It is broken only by fine contact lines, which
give the building the appearance of an elaborately perforated monolith. It was perfected during the planning
phase until the greatest possible precision had been at-
tained. The solution that was found is a combination of
the shingle and tongue-and-groove principles that con-
ceals the method of assembly. The joints between the
copper sheets virtually disappear. The window sills are
designed in a similar way to minimize their susceptibility
to soiling. The absolutely plane sheet metal façade, realized with millimetre precision, required the production
of 164 cutting patterns. The copper is prepatinated to
initiate the natural aging process.

06

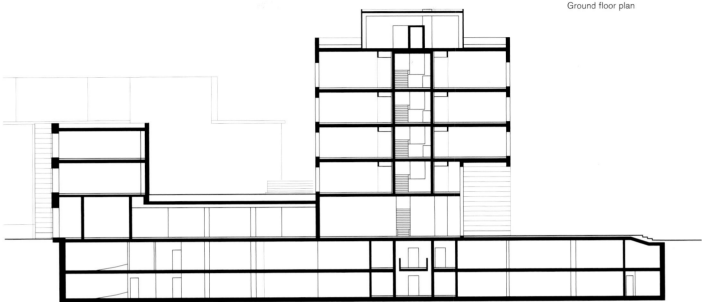

01 Night view Kaistraße **02** Entrance with forecourt **03 + 04** View into the roof garden **05** Window detail **06** Cross section **07** Ground floor plan

07

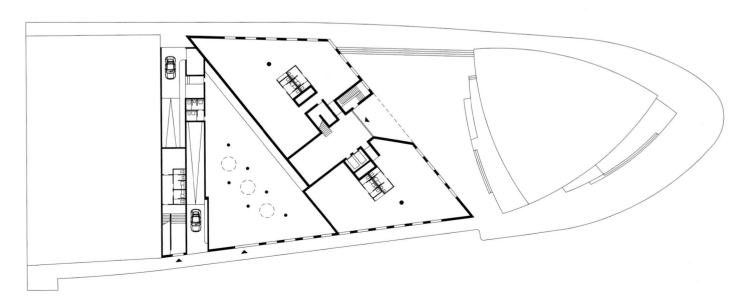

Lentos Kunstmuseum, 2003
Address: Lentos Museum of Modern Art, Ernst-Koref-Promenade 1, 4020 Linz, Austria. **Gross floor area:** 7,700 m². **Materials:** concrete, glass, metal, wood, poured asphalt.

On the blue Danube
ARCHITECTS: Weber Hofer Partner AG

The Lentos Museum marks the western end of the Danube Park and follows the line of the high-water dam. Like a beached ship it lies along the banks of the Danube, encircled on one side by water, on the other surrounded by the park. Two small concrete cubes housing the exits of the underground car-park protrude like basalt taps on the city side of the museum and anchor the voluminous glass "ship". A particularly impressive feature is the open sculpture hall within the body of the edifice. This pillar-free space, 60 by 24 metres large, it is as much an urban space as an entrance hall to the museum and acts as a meeting place for visitors to the museum and the park. At the same time it is a window on the Danube. Looking through the building, the visitor glimpses the Danube and Urfahr district with the magnificent silhouette of the Pöstling mountain. The glass enclosure is supported by a filigree metal structure that is scarcely visible by day and revealed by back-lighting at night.

03

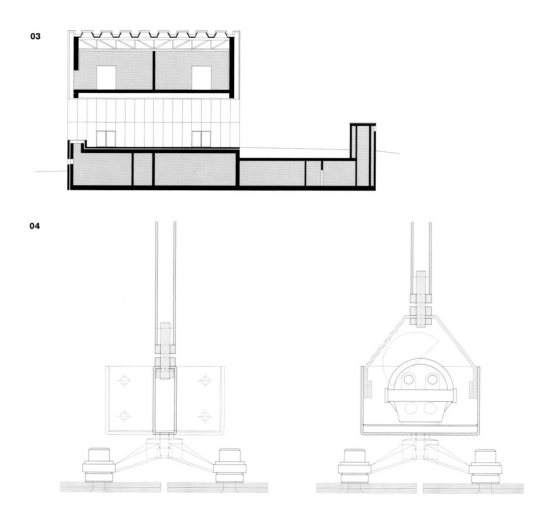

04

05

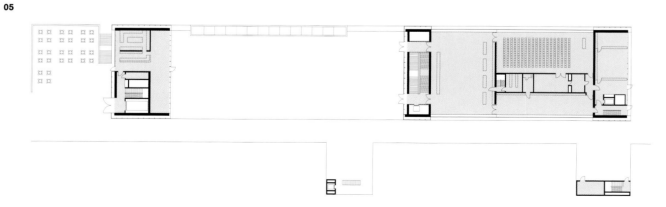

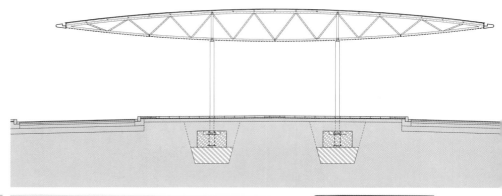

Central bus station, Herne, 2004
Address: Konrad-Adenauer-Platz, 44629 Herne, Germany. **Client:** Straßenbahn Herne-Castrop-Rauxel GmbH, Gebäudemanagement Herne GMH. **Gross floor area:** roof area approx. 3,100 m². **Materials:** steel, glass, stainless steel, aluminium.

Stainless steel in the city of coal
ARCHITECTS:
HEIDERICH HUMMERT KLEIN Architekten
(today Heiderich Hummert, Dortmund)

Covering the bus stop island and supported by two parallel rows of columns is a transparent roof in the shape of two ellipses, fused lengthwise. The convex roof structure, with its upper surface of clear glass, fine stainless steel fabric underlay and clad-clad rounded edges, is bathed in a soft green glow during the hours of darkness. The transparent complement of glass and stainless steel creates a friendly, cheerful atmosphere and gives passengers a sense of orientation and security in this newly designed bus station. Silver trussed girders clad underneath in woven stainless steel give the roof its elegant lightness, making it appear as though it were a transparent, floating unit.

01 Cross section **02** Western view of the north edge **03** Aerial view **04** Night view with artwork "Cube Crack"

Quayside granary warehouse on the river port in Harburg, 2004
Address: Nartenstraße 1 / Am Veritaskai, 21079 Hamburg, Germany. **General planning:** Lindschulte + Partner Planungsgesellschaft GmbH (authorization and final planning of the façade). **Client:** Lorenz Vogler GbR. **Site supervision:** Lindschulte + Partner Planungsgesellschaft GmbH. **Engineers:** Lindschulte + Partner Planungsgesellschaft GmbH. **Gross floor area:** 1,700 m². **Materials:** reinforced concrete, Alucobond façade.

Harbour flair and high-tech
ARCHITECTS:
André Poitiers Architekt RIBA Stadtplaner
(design of façade and defining details)

The river port in Hamburg has experienced an unexpected renaissance in recent years. Many of the empty warehouses have been converted to new uses, while new office buildings and laboratories have also been added. The two oldest sections of the old quayside granary warehouse (Kaispeicher) have been retained. The Kaispeicher was originally built between 1928 and 1961. The feed hoppers of the silo bins and the grain conveyer now stand in the entrance foyer as reminders of its original use. Floor slabs have been inserted into this 30-metre-high cellular-structured building in order to provide new office spaces. A extension in concrete, glass and steel sets a fresh architectural tone in a district otherwise dominated by brick – high tech on the waterfront. Because the north side of the building faces the water, it was decided to maximise the amount of glass in this façade, creating a workplace with harbour flair.

03

01 Façade detail **02** View from the harbour **03** Longitudinal section **04** Ground floor plan **05** View from the street **06** Façade

04

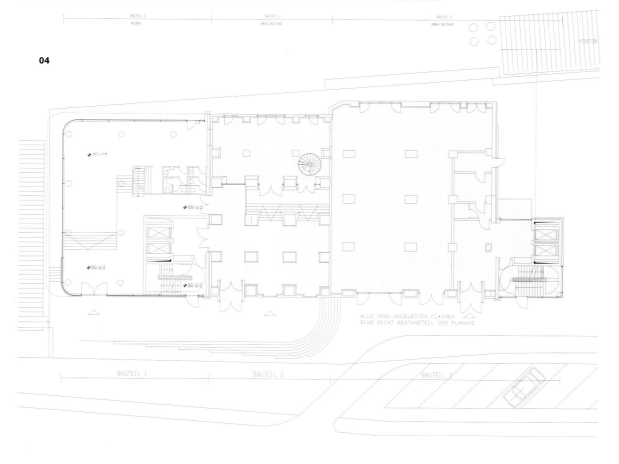

76

Galway-Mayo IT Learning Resource Centre, 2003
Address: Dublin Road, Galway, Ireland. **Client:** Galway-Mayo Institute of Technology. **Total floor area:** 10,262 m². **Materials:** Irish limestone, pigmented render, patinated copper.

Significant and identifiable form
ARCHITECTS: Murray Ó Laoire Architects

The building is split into two distinct volumes; lecture theatres and the library/IT department. The lecture theatre volume is clad with rendered concrete blocks while the south elevation of the library/IT block is clad in limestone with pre-patinated free form compositions that reflect the shape of trapezoidal sails and takes cognisance of Galway's location on the shores of the Atlantic Ocean and it's maritime past. The copper "sails" act as large air dispensers, and form part of the library natural ventilation strategy providing fresh air to the library area by "Stack Effect", by cross ventilation. The library interior reflects the organic external forms. Racked columns push "islands" of floor plane towards the sails. The floor plane fractures to create trapezoidal voids through which light filters to the lower library floor. The design uses architectural elements as orientation devices, the building form to zone its functions, its skin to control the environment, and the use of materials as a hierarchical index.

04

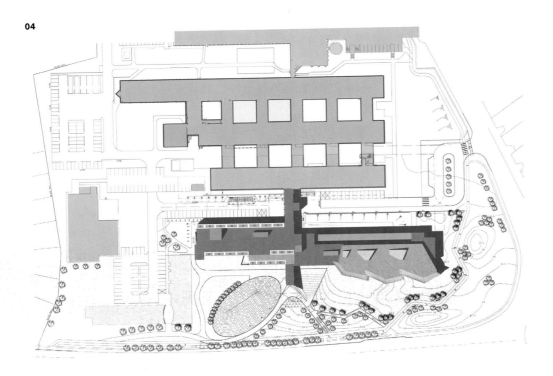

01 Night view of library's prepatinated copper "sails" **02** Interior view library **03** Exterior view of library's prepatinated copper "sails" by day **04** Campus site plan **05** Section through library / IT centre **06** Learning Centre foyer / main entrance **07** View of library's reading area

05

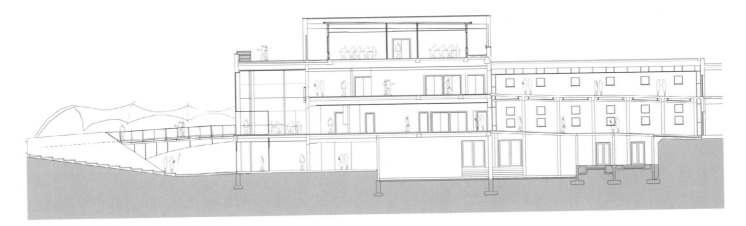

Südwestmetall Reutlingen, 2003
Address: Schulstraße 23, Reutlingen, Germany.
Client: Südwestmetall, Verband der Metall- und Elektroindustrie Baden-Württemberg e. V. **Gross floor area:** 4,200 m² (including underground car-park).
Materials: stainless steel.

Corporate architecture
ARCHITECTS:
Allmann Sattler Wappner Architekten

Simple in shape but complex in its realisation, the design of these buildings reconciles local building regulations with Südwestmetall's desire to express its identity as the metal industry federation for the state of Baden-Württemberg. The gable roofs invoke both the existing building as well as the traditional architecture of this area of Reutlingen, while the metal cubes are a significant outward representation of the user's identity. The surfaces consist of two differently worked metals. A latticework of cast-steel elements forms the ground-floor exterior and façade and alludes to the wrought-iron trelliswork of the adjacent building. Filled with aggregate and earth, the ornamentation, which is mainly used on the ground surfaces, is continued vertically on the base façades and as a screen in front of the glass façade. The upper floors are clad in smooth, flat stainless steel plating that opens up in the window areas.

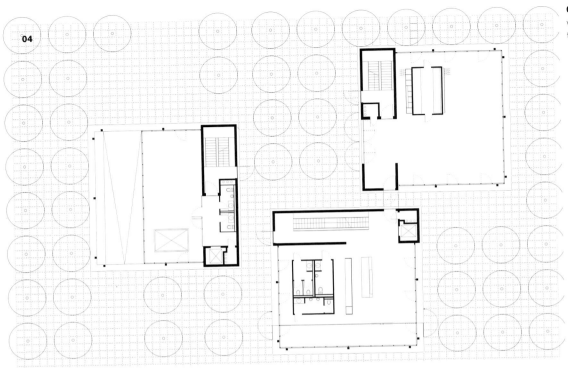

04

01 Entrance area **02** + **03** Exterior view **04** Ground floor plan **05** Section **06** Entrance **07** Exterior view

05

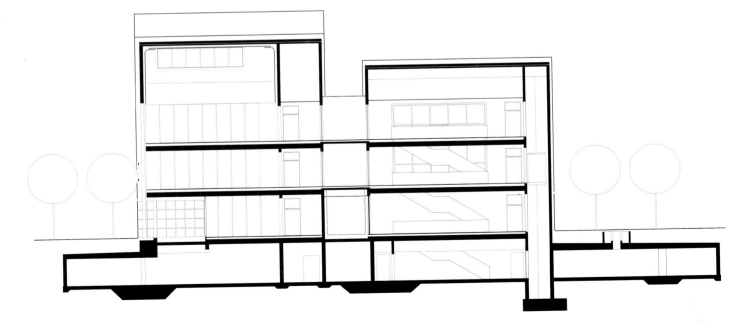

84

Hessing cockpit building in an acoustic barrier, 2005
Address: Leidsche Rijn Utrecht, The Netherlands.
Client: Hessing Holding BV. **Gross floor area:** 6,400 m².

Non standard architecture
ARCHITECTS: ONL [Oosterhuis_Lénárd]

This project is a classic example of Non-Standard Architecture realized on a grand scale. The basic principle behind NSA is that all components are essentially different. The exception proves the rule. If two components are similar, this is accidental and not relevant. But all exceptions are found in a rigidly defined parametric design system. The adage "one building, one detail" applies here. NSA is based on the new industrial production method of mass customisation. Non-Standard Architecture is the architecture of smooth transition. The geometric engineering was conducted in-house at ONL. The architects were fully responsible for the exact data on the tens of thousands of integrated elements. For this purpose ONL programmed an effective file to factory process through the writing of project specific scripts. The scripts describe the geometry exactly and the data is registered in a database. This data is read by the software controlling the production machinery.

05

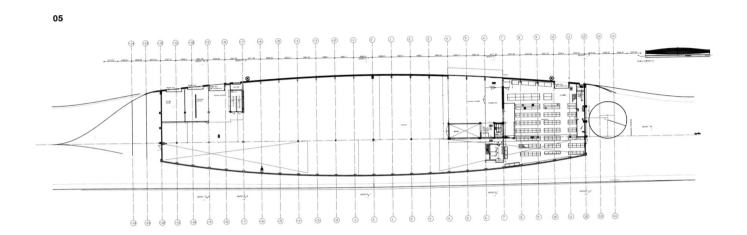

06

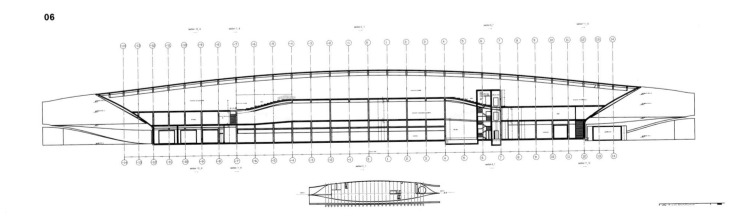

Slender/Bender, 2004
Address: Hessische Str. 5, Berlin, Germany.
Client: Jürgens, Jürgens, Griffin GbR. **Gross floor
area:** 560 m².

Slender and Bender
ARCHITECTS: Deadline
Britta Jürgens, Matthew Griffin

This project combines short-term "Miniloft" apartments, offices, a single-family home, a shop and car-
park. "Slender/Bender" is an expansive gesture within
a confined space. The building was constructed in two
phases. The renovation and refurbishment work on the
existing building (Slender) was completed in 2002. This
side wing was then completely transformed in 2004
with the addition of the new structure (Bender), which
also forms the access portal to Slender. Three curved
stainless steel bands embrace the old building behind
and mediate between the neighbouring buildings on
either side. The building thus grows out of the past but
aspires to a futuristic dynamism with its forward tilting
gesture. The distinctive stainless steel bands reflect
and abstract the surrounding colours and movements.
Its mixture of conforming and reflecting colours, and
nonconforming shapes and materials make this building oddly inconspicuous while at the same time strong
and distinctive.

03

04

05

06

07

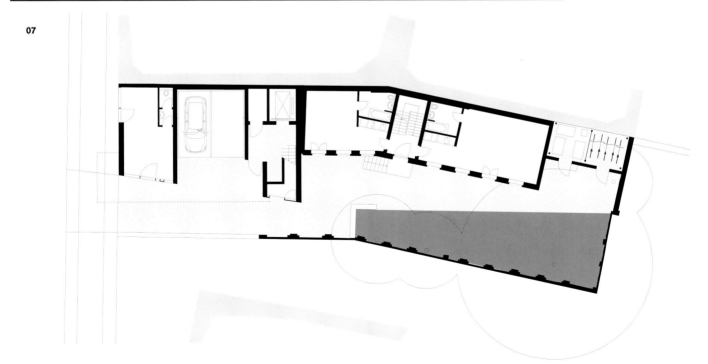

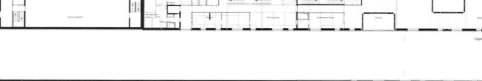

Training centre with cafeteria, 2005
Address: Straße der Freundschaft 13, 01904 Neukirch, Germany. **Client:** TRUMPF Sachsen GmbH. **Gross floor area:** 2,350 m².

Time-Line
ARCHITECTS: Barkow Leibinger Architekten, Berlin

Three architectural elements were amalgamated into a new entity on the site of a machine tool factory in Neukirch (Saxony): the production shed built in 1900, an extension from the 1980s and a 30-metre-long new building, which extends the longitudinal axis of the property to a total of 115 metres. The façades and roof have a uniform cladding of anthracite grey zinc shingle. The use of shingle and the punched wooden windows are derived from local architectural tradition. A large seminar room and a cafeteria to seat 120 are located on the top floor under the 45-degree pitched roof. The building is thus the social hub of the company site. The roof soffit is characterised by large-format prefabricated timber sections supported by a steel frame structure. Several small scale houses have been built into the space for the kitchen and storerooms and cut out as terraces.

01 Upper floor plan, ground floor plan and cross section **02** Dining space with cut-out terraces **03** North west elevation

94

Kontor 19 in Rheinauhafen, Cologne, 2005
Address: Kontor 19 Rheinauhafen Cologne, Anna-Schneider-Steig 8–10, 50678 Cologne, Germany. **Gross floor area:** 7,230 m².

The gilded look
ARCHITECTS:
GATERMANN + SCHOSSIG, Cologne

In terms of urban development, this simple, homogenous structure in the Rheinauhafen area of Cologne is located between the listed Hafenamt (port authority) and the historical Bayenturm tower. The striking effect of the new building derives primarily from the tense contrast between the solid aluminium panels and the transparent glass panels of the multifunctional façade. What is distinctive about the aluminium panels, which were manufactured in New Zealand, is their graphic composition. A special process involving etching and anodising was used to engrave the panels, giving the building a different appearance depending on the time of day, the weather and the viewing angle, turning it from dark grey to gold. To further enhance the visual unity of the structure with its completely flat shell, the solid façade elements are covered with an organic crystalline pattern. Depending on the vantage point, a completely variable image is created by the scratchy graphic pattern, allowing the surface to be perceived in different ways.

01 Façade 02 Kontor 19 with historical Bayenturm 03 Kontor 19 between Hafenamt and the historical Bayenturm 04 Aluminium panel 05 Ground floor plan 06 Façade section 07 Stepped storey 08 Interior

05

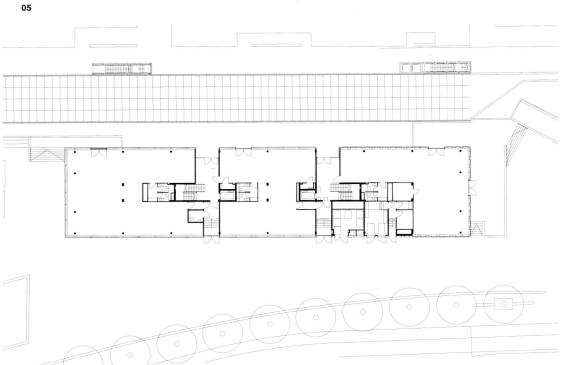

06

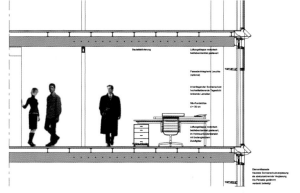

Elektro Graf extension, 2003
Address: Dornbirn, Austria. **Client:** Ing. Elmar Graf, Dornbirn, Austria. **Total floor area:** 1,908 m².
Materials: pre-patinated copper sheet, antisun glazing (Parsol green), reinforced concrete, plasterboard, natural rubber.

Playful harmony

ARCHITECTS: Baumschlager-Eberle
Ziviltechniker GmbH

This building is a testament to the architectural culture of Vorarlberg, Austria's westernmost province, and to an architect who was not afraid to create a clear, modern and geometric design in an Alpine environment. And to an alter ego, the client, that permitted this. The electronics company has added a cube to its complex, a structure that shimmers green or reflects its surrounding depending on the weather. Towering above everything else is a high-bay warehouse, which together with the first new building and a connecting passage creates a new courtyard. The chosen material: copper. The new sections form a deliberate contrast to the older ones, and nevertheless the architects manage to express a feeling of playful harmony with the ensemble.

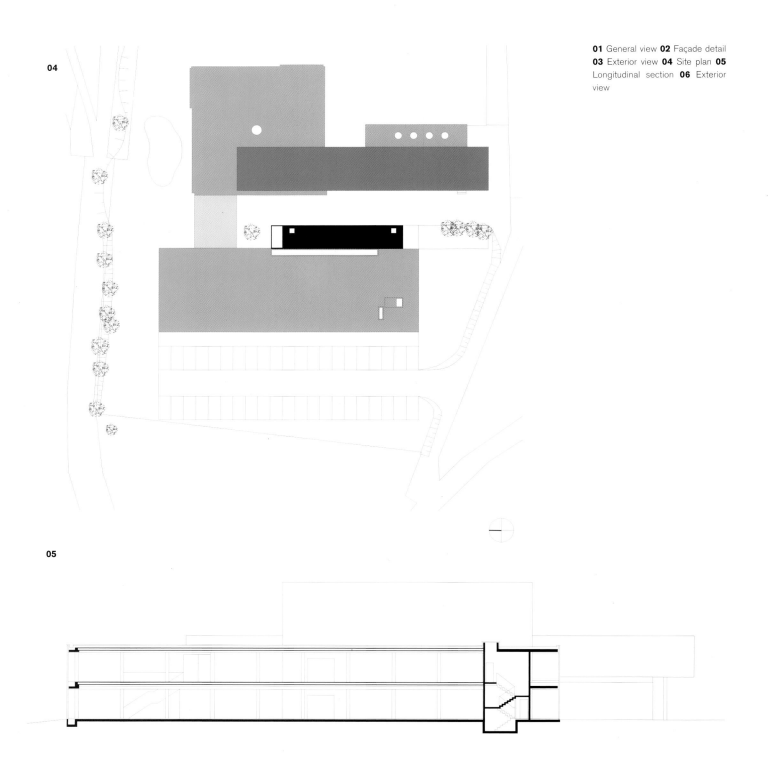

04

01 General view **02** Façade detail
03 Exterior view **04** Site plan **05**
Longitudinal section **06** Exterior
view

05

Expansion of the "Klosterschule" school in Hamburg, 2006
Address: Westphalensweg 7, 20099 Hamburg, Germany. **Client:** City of Hamburg represented by the Public Education Authority. **Gross floor area:** 1,207 m². **Materials:** masonry, concrete, glass, steel, wood, electrochemically treated stainless sheet as curtain façade.

An exciting contrast
ARCHITECTS:
THÜS FARNSCHLÄDER ARCHITEKTEN

No less a figure than Fritz Schumacher (Hamburg's chief building director from 1909 to 1934) built this school (named after the Klostertor district in which it is located), which was expanded in 1995. The new building takes up from this construction phase and connects directly to the old building via a bridge. The resulting L-shaped ensemble is grouped around the schoolyard and sports ground along the continued, strict axes of the old structure. In addition to classrooms, a new large kitchen, a dining room, and rooms for leisure activities have been created. The modern stainless steel and glass façade blends in well with the original clinker brick, at the same time producing an exciting contrast. The electrochemically treated stainless sheet functions as a curtain wall, and its solidity and weight contrast with the lightness of the ribbon windows. It gives the building its clear horizontal pattern and particular appearance, while its colour matches the clinker.

04

05

06

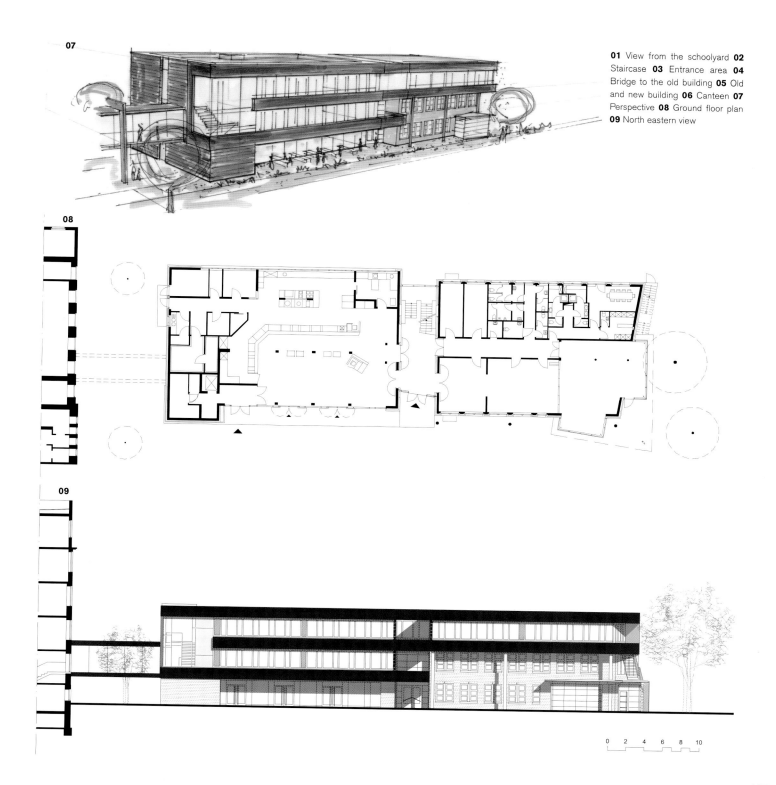

07

08

09

0 2 4 6 8 10

Conversion and refurbishment of Jakobstraße bower, 2006
Address: Eiermarkt 1a, 38100 Braunschweig, Germany. **Client:** Karin and Joachim Prüsse. **Materials:** Corten steel.

Link between new and old

ARCHITECTS: O.M. Architekten BDA
Rainer Ottinger, Thomas Möhlendick

Germany's medieval cities are getting more dignified treatment these days. Gone are the days of urban renewal or demolition, or for that matter the vulgar reconstruction of surviving ruins. In Braunschweig a new structure has been inserted between the historic castle bower and the Jakobskirche. A new interval space has thereby been created that is reminiscent of the city's past. What has been created is a small, tasteful event and coaching centre. A glass-fronted entrance section forms the link between the old and new structures. Corten steel plates cover the wall and roof surfaces of the new building. These plates vary in size and were combined with window openings in such a way as to convey the feel of a medieval city – something one experiences here in small doses only.

01 Library **02** Aerial view **03** View
from the market place (Eiermarkt)
04 Elevation **05** Ground floor plan
06 Second floor plan **07** Foyer,
view of the new building

04

05

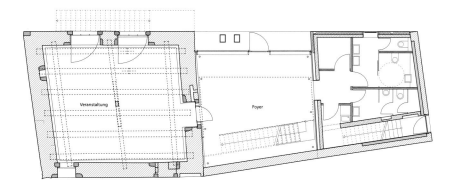

06

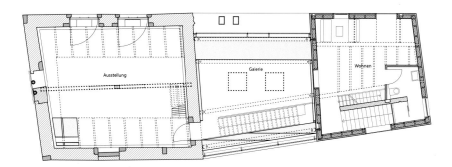

01

Relaxation Park in Torrevieja, 2007
Address: Torrevieja, Valencia, Spain. **Structural engineers:** Sasaki and Partners + Masahiro Ikeda Architecture Studio, Augustin Obiol (Obiol & Moya Arquitectes Associates, S. C. P.). **Architects involved:** Jose Maria Torres Nadal, Antonio Marquerie Tamayo, Joaquín Albado Bañon, Ken-ichi Shinozaki **Client:** Torrevieja City. **Gross floor area:** 1,245 m².

Following the landscape
ARCHITECTS: Toyo Ito & Associates, Architects

Located just inland from the coast are two lakes that can be described as symbols of the town. One of the lakes has a beautiful pink colour. The colour of this mysterious lake seems to change from moment to moment; this is said to be the effect of high salt concentrations and bacteria in the water. Mud from the lake and lake shore is beneficial for thalassotherapy, and those who wish to enjoy its therapeutic powers flock to this area. The shell plans were generated by Bezier curves that follow the landscape, and in cross section the ratio of the ellipse was derived from the length of the major axis. The spiral weaves together five steel rods (60 mm diameter) linked by timber joists (180 x 90) that span 4.5–5.5 metres, thus creating the external form of the shell. Some parts of the exterior are enclosed with plywood, resulting in a soft exoskeleton structure similar to that of a living creature. Although the floors are hung from the spiral structure, they give the structure additional rigidity and stability by connecting the five steel rods. In this way, all of the components function as structural elements and thus contribute to the whole.

01 Under construction (July, 2004) **02** Arch plans **03** Model **04** CG image

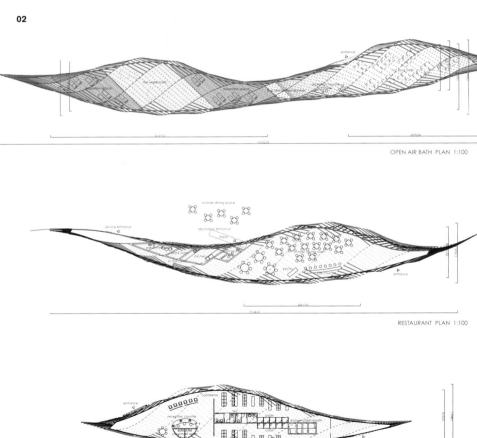

02

OPEN AIR BATH PLAN 1:100

RESTAURANT PLAN 1:100

INFORMATION OFFICE PLAN 1:100

112

AS16 Suncatcher, 2006
Address: Am Sandbach 16, Gardessen bei Braunschweig, Germany. **Client:** Haus Metzner GmbH & Co. KG. **Materials:** "TECU Gold" copper alloy.

 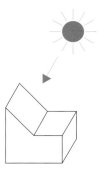 

Capturing the sun
ARCHITECTS: m3xh . Jörg Baumeister

As part of a reconstruction project, a new entrance was created for a senior citizens' residence. The architect's proposal was both unusual and captivating: an emblematic combination of cube and lean-to roof, clad with a copper surface of gleaming shingle. "Capturing the sun" is how the architect describes the primary design principle; the south-facing glazed roof produces a shadow play in the interior. Outside, the appearance of the façade is determined by the play of sun- and moonlight, causing it to alternately shimmer, sparkle, blaze, dazzle or gleam. Gradually the surface will also acquire a matt patina. The reflective properties of the façade ("TECU Gold" copper alloy) show the constantly changing direction of light, the spectral energy distribution and the diffusion of light to full effect.

01 Finding the form **02** Entrance view **03** South façade

02

**"Industrial Culture Workshop" Göttelborn
Coal Mine, 2005**
Address: Boulevard der Industriekultur, 66287 Göttelborn, Germany. **Client:** Government of the State of Saarland, represented by Industriekultur Saar GmbH. **Gross floor area:** 2600 m². **Materials:** reinforced concrete, steel, aluminium, polycarbonate.

A symbol of continuity
ARCHITECTS: Augustin und Frank Architekten

On the site of a former coal mine, the former pithead baths and electronics workshop were converted into a company headquarters, exhibition and event spaces and offices. A small guest house was also added. Because most of the original buildings were light structures that were built to house machinery, the intention here was to emulate these thin-layered structures in the shells of the new buildings. Therefore, principally those materials and construction techniques used in industrial buildings were applied in the reconstruction and refitting work. Even the newly built guest house reflects this principle: with its visually stunning, layered façade of perforated, trapezoidal aluminium sheet, it stands out conspicuously as a symbol of continuity.

01

02

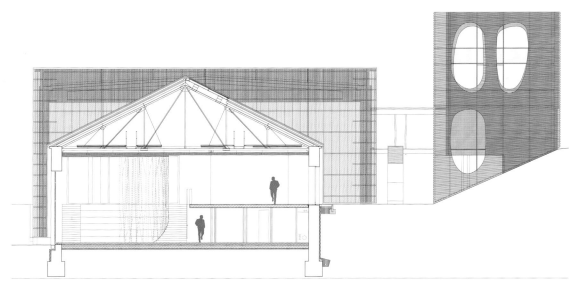

06

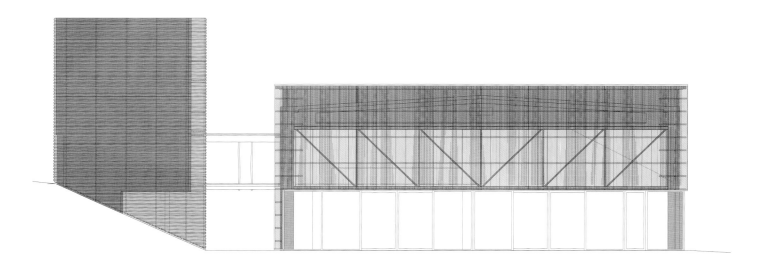

118

Main auditorium of Brandenburg University of Applied Sciences, 2006
Address: Magdeburger Straße 53, 14770 Brandenburg, Germany. **Gross floor area:** 1,292 m². **Materials:** clinker brick (repair work), steel, glass, Corten steel, smoked oak.

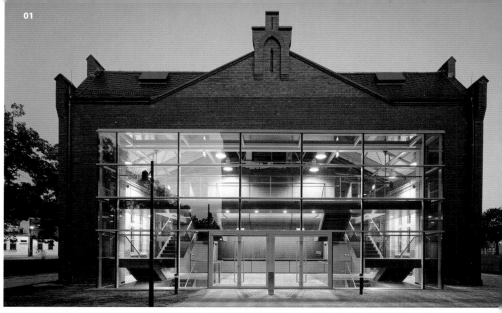

A history of steel
ARCHITECTS: Reiner Becker, Potsdam

With a new-old slate roof the hall regained its old look into which the new has been implanted. In a homage to Brandenburg's history as a city of steel the visitor is met at the foyer by a vision of steel: two elegant steel staircases and a control booth encased in Corten steel that overhangs the cloakroom. From the foyer students pass through a glass partition and enter an auditorium with telescopic tiered seating for 300 people. All of the built-in units are painted in metallic monochrome. This allows the large space, the old masonry, the steel beams and two Corten steel structures to achieve their full effect. The building services, heating, acoustics, lighting and ventilation of this partially air-conditioned space have been effectively concentrated within the stage area and the roof structure. The key factors that needed to be considered in the redevelopment of this auditorium were its history and current use. The history of the Brandenburg region as a location for the steel industry and a military stronghold had to be balanced against the high-tech vision of the future represented by the university. This manifests in a playful agglomeration of different structures and designs, masking high-tech elements.

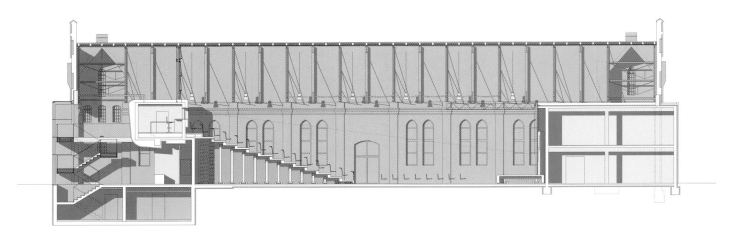

05

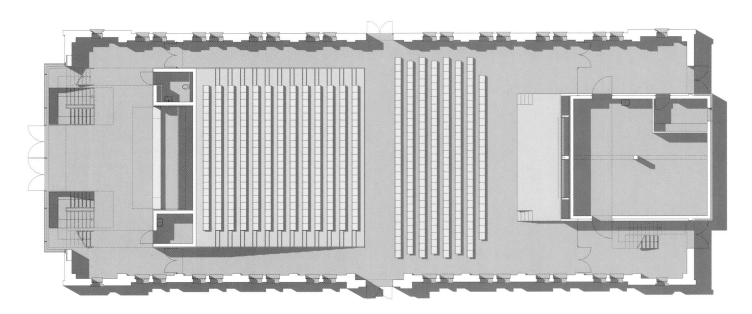

Rolandsbrücke office building, Hamburg, 2005
Headquarter Norddeutsche Vermögen
Address: Rolandsbrücke 4, 20095 Hamburg, Germany.
Client: Dr. Bernd Kortüm, c/o Norddeutsche Grund-
vermögen. **Gross floor area:** 4,500 m². **Materials:**
aluminium / expanded metal, glass.

Innovative shell
ARCHITECTS: CARSTEN ROTH ARCHITEKT

This office building on the Rolandsbrücke is one of the
pillars of the "gateway" to the old city of Hamburg. This
ten-storey new building blends in well with an ensemble
of late-nineteenth century and post-war architecture.
The building achieves this thanks to its height and the
sculptural work on the body and façade. Projections
and recesses, the separate design of the upper floors
along Brodschrangen street and the horizontal and vertical surfaces of the neighbouring building combine to
harmoniously integrate this building into its surroundings. It is thus simultaneously a solitary, semi-detached,
heightened and corner building. The cubist-like tilted
sculptural structure wears a decorative three-dimen-
sional netted gown that was designed uniquely by the
Hamburg architect Carsten Roth. Between the windows
expanded mesh panels catch the sunlight, their oppos-
ing triangle pattern producing a relief-like effect. In the
shifting light of evening this cool façade reveals an unexpected vivacity.

01

01 Staircase **02** Façade Neß /
Große Reichenstraße **03** First floor
plan, conference level **04** 8th floor
plan **05** Corner view Neß / Brodschrangen **06** View from Dom-
straße

03

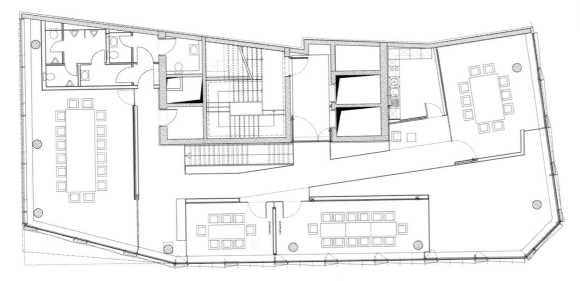

04

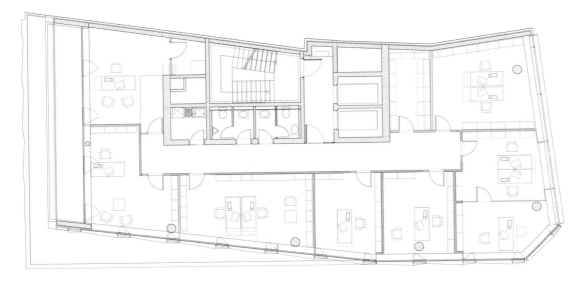

Headquarters of Fanuc Robotics Deutschland, 2004
Office / administrative building, exhibition and training centre
Address: Bernhäuser Straße 36, 73765 Neuhausen a.d.F., Germany. **Client:** Fanuc Robotics Deutschland GmbH. **Gross floor area:** approx. 7,750 m². **Materials:** steel, glass, aluminium, bankirai wood.

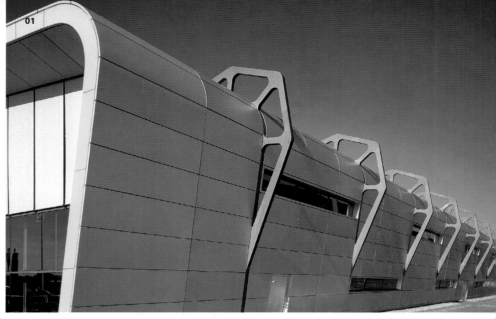

Branding at a glance
ARCHITECTS: Gewers Kühn und Kühn, Berlin

Fanuc Robotics is a Japanese company with global reach. The architecture and structural design of the German headquarters were inspired by the corporate identity (e.g. the colour yellow, high-tech products, efficiency). The prototype in Neuhausen near Stuttgart (to be followed by further projects in other countries) is based on three "tracks". The length and height of these tracks vary and all run from south to north. The lightweight and spacious eastern "track" is column-free and provides demonstration and modification facilities. The multi-storey western "track" contains storage as well as training and administrative areas. The two are linked by the third "track", which acts as an access and delivery spine. Thanks to a figure-hugging skin of shiny anodised aluminium, large glass frontage and the illuminated border in the corporate colour yellow this is a building that truly makes its mark.

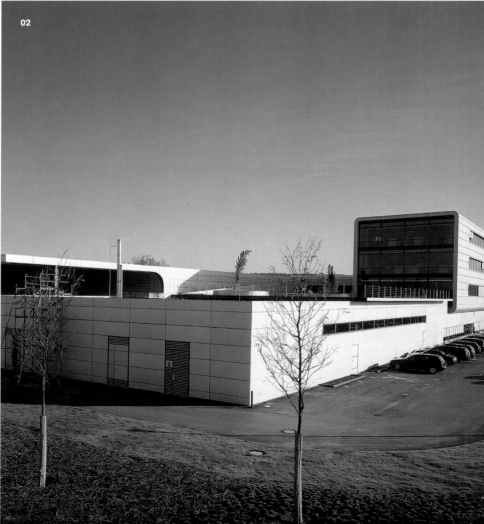

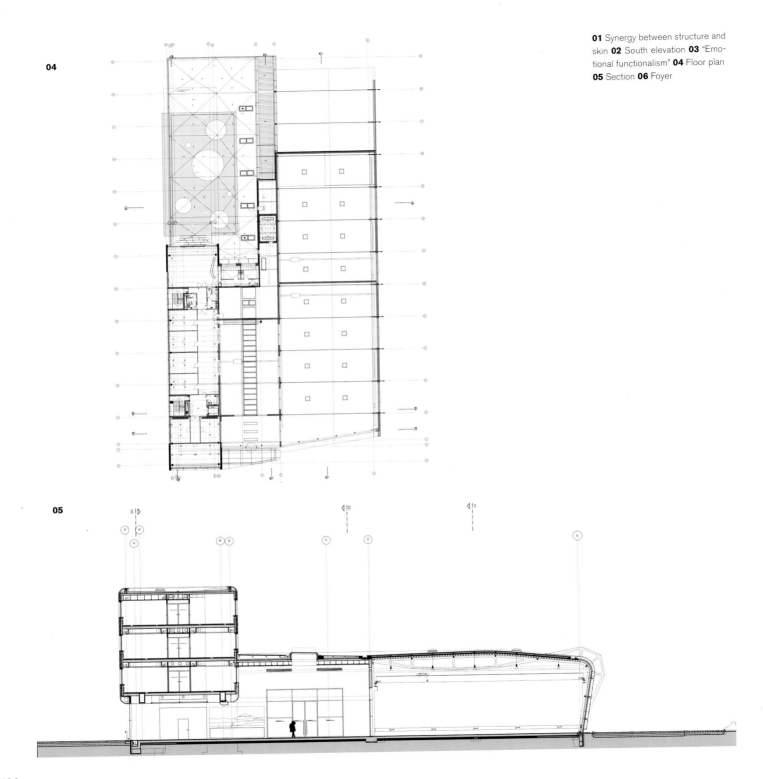

04

05

01 Synergy between structure and skin **02** South elevation **03** "Emotional functionalism" **04** Floor plan **05** Section **06** Foyer

Palestra Office Building, 2006
Address: Southwark Underground Station, London,
United Kingdom. **Client:** Blackfriars Investments.
Gross floor area: 25,000 m².

A raised box
ARCHITECTS: SMC ALSOP, London

The opening of the Tate Modern combined with improved
communications – the Jubilee Line Extension and Alsop's
forthcoming Thameslink 2000 station at Blackfriars (with
links to Luton and Gatwick airports) – have made the
Bankside district south of the Thames potentially one of
the most dynamic cultural and commercial growth points
of London. The key idea behind the bold speculative
Palestra commercial scheme is the provision of large,
straightforward and highly flexible floor plates, which can
be used in open plan or cellular formats. The building
takes the form of a raised box, with retail and restaurant
space at ground level, where public routes penetrate the
development. The offices are arranged in two distinct
planes, separated by an open level of "social space". The
appearance of the building belies its basically simple dia-
gram. The façades make use of the most advanced glazing technology, with benefits not only in terms of working
environment and climatic controls but also in terms of
the aesthetics of the building. The glazing incorporates
a bold abstract pattern that is impermeably bonded into
the individual glass sheets – and thus becomes a huge
artwork challenging the prejudice that speculative office
space is visually boring or environmentally negative.

03

04

01 Façade detail 02 View from the street 03 Floor plan, ground level 04 Elevation 05 View from the neighbouring building

03

04

7500 7500 7500 7500 7500 7500 7500 7500 7500 7500 7500 7500

Aa A B C D E F G H I J K L M

area for curtain walling mock up

area for curtain walling mock up

area for curtain walling mock up

Xeros Residence, 2006
Address: 1441 East Sunnyside Drive, Phoenix, Arizona 85020, USA. **Client:** Matthew + Lisa Trzebiatowski.
Gross floor area: 153.3 m² – conditioned spaces.
Materials: unfinished corrugated steel cladding; clear, colour-laminated and colour-tinted glass; unfinished woven steel wire mesh shade screens.

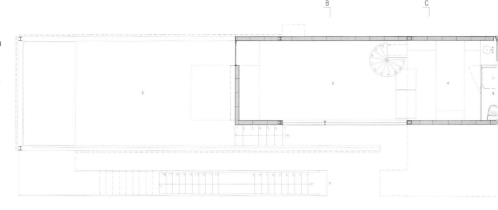

In the desert
ARCHITECTS: blank studio

Called "Xeros" (from the Greek for "dry") as a reminder that all design solutions should be in a direct response to the environment in which the project exists, the building contains several environmentally responsible decisions. The form turns an opaque face towards the intense western afternoon sun and its more exposed faces to the south and east are shielded by an external layer of woven metal shade mesh. The long, narrow site allows the maximum amount of space to be retained for vegetation. The low-water-use vegetation is positioned around the residence to add to the shading effect of the screen. The site itself was "recycled" in that new life was injected into a neglected plot in a neglected Phoenix neighbourhood. The primary building material is exposed steel (as structure, cladding, and shading) that is allowed to weather naturally and meld with the colour of the surrounding hills.

01 Mezzanine level floor plan **02** Northern view of the studio level
03 View of northern façade **04** Detail of eastern façade

School of Art & Art History, University of Iowa, 2006
Address: Iowa City, Iowa, USA. **Design architects:** Steven Holl, Chris McVoy, Martin Cox **Client:** University of Iowa. **Gross floor area:** 6,500 m².

A hybrid vision of the future
ARCHITECTS:

Steven Holl Architects, New York

The site presented special conditions: an existing 1937 brick building with a central body and flanking wings located along the Iowa River in addition to two existing morphologies; a lagoon and a connection to the organic geometry of nearby limestone bluffs that form the edge of the Iowa City grid. The new building straddles these two morphologies. The new School of Art and Art History is a hybrid instrument of open edges and open centre; instead of an object, the building is a "formless" instrument. Implied rather than actual volumes are outlined in the disposition of spaces. Flat or curved planes are slotted together or assembled with hinged sections. Flexible spaces open out from studios in warm weather. The main horizontal passages are meeting places with interior glass walls that reveal work in progress. The interplay of light is controlled through shading created by the overlapping planar exterior. The resulting architecture is a hybrid vision of the future, combining bridge and loft spaces, theory with practice and human requirements with scientific principles.

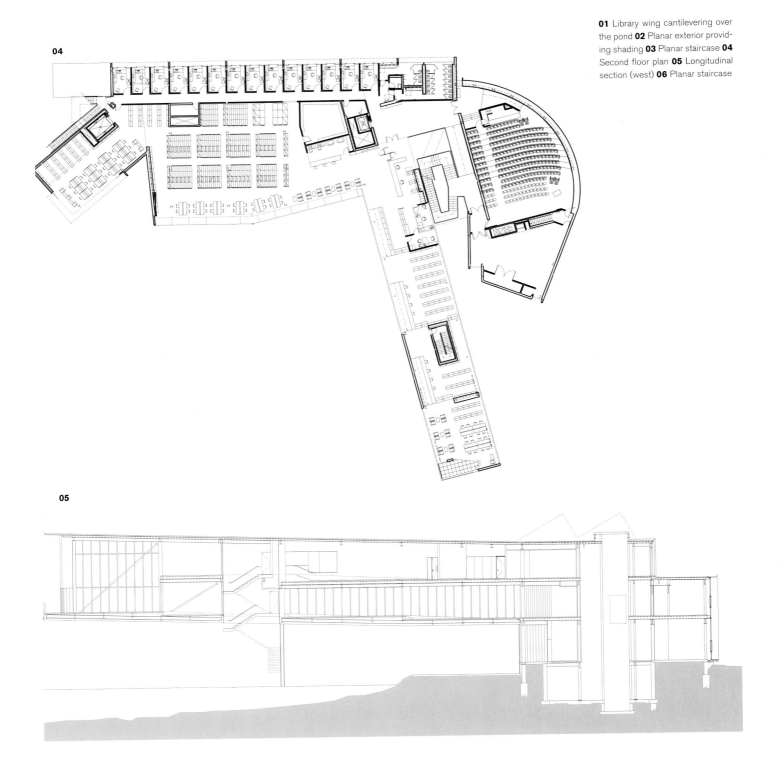

04

01 Library wing cantilevering over the pond **02** Planar exterior providing shading **03** Planar staircase **04** Second floor plan **05** Longitudinal section (west) **06** Planar staircase

05

SCULPTURE

Marqués de Riscal Hotel, 2006
Address: Calle Torrea 1, 01340 Elciego, Spain. **Client:** Marqués de Riscal Hotel. **Materials:** 1,800 m² of tinted titanium imported from Japan; 1,750 m² of stainless steel; 1,200 m² of curtain walling; 3,180 m² of metallic canopies.

Little Bilbao
ARCHITECTS: Frank O. Gehry

The central part of this complex is the building designed by Frank O. Gehry, which will house the company headquarters and hotel complex. The result is an ambitious project that combines state-of-the-art architecture, local landscape and enjoyment of the culture and essence of wine. A mix of modernity and tradition, the Marqués de Riscal Hotel is Gehry's homage to this vine-growing region. Thus the building appears to rise from the land like a great vine. The building is particularly characterised by its form and use of materials. Gehry chose materials and forms similar to those used in the Bilbao Guggenheim Museum, although in this case the titanium covering – the Canadian architect's trademark – are in the colours of Marqués de Riscal; pink representing wine, gold the mesh that covers the bottle and silver the bottle cap.

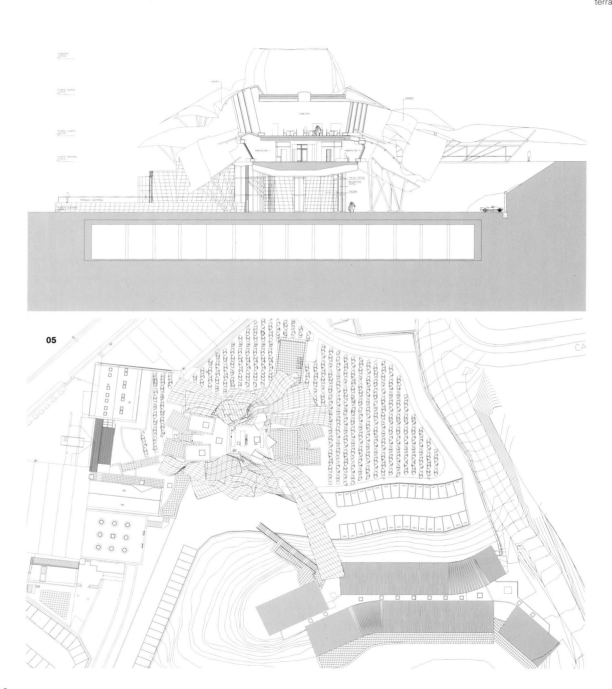

05

Popstage Mezz, 2002
Address: Keizerstraat 101, 4811 HL Breda,
The Netherlands. **Client:** Municipality of Breda.
Gross floor area: 1,600 m² (incl. 720 m² new building).
Materials: copper (outer shell), wood (inner shell).

Like a ferry
ARCHITECTS:
(EEA) Erick van Egeraat associated architects

As part of the urban development scheme for the aban-
doned "Chassée" military campus in Breda, designed
by the Office of Metropolitan Architecture, the former
officers' canteen was converted into a venue for Breda's many lovers of pop music. Located at the south
west corner of the site, this building, dating from 1899,
is centered on the inner area of the former barracks
grounds. The extension, located on the other side of the
old canteen, accommodates the concert hall and foyer.
It is shaped like a voluptuous seashell that adjoins the
existing structure. Where the old and new buildings
meet, an opening is created. The skeleton of the outer
shell is a hybrid structure of steel and concrete that for
acoustic reasons is covered by a 100-mm skin of poured
concrete and a pre-oxidized copper. All entrances to the
new extension are hidden by the skin of the outer shell.
Only when the doors actually open does the shell reveal
its penetrability. The 3-by-4-metre steel frame door of
the dock shelter opens dramatically like a car ferry.

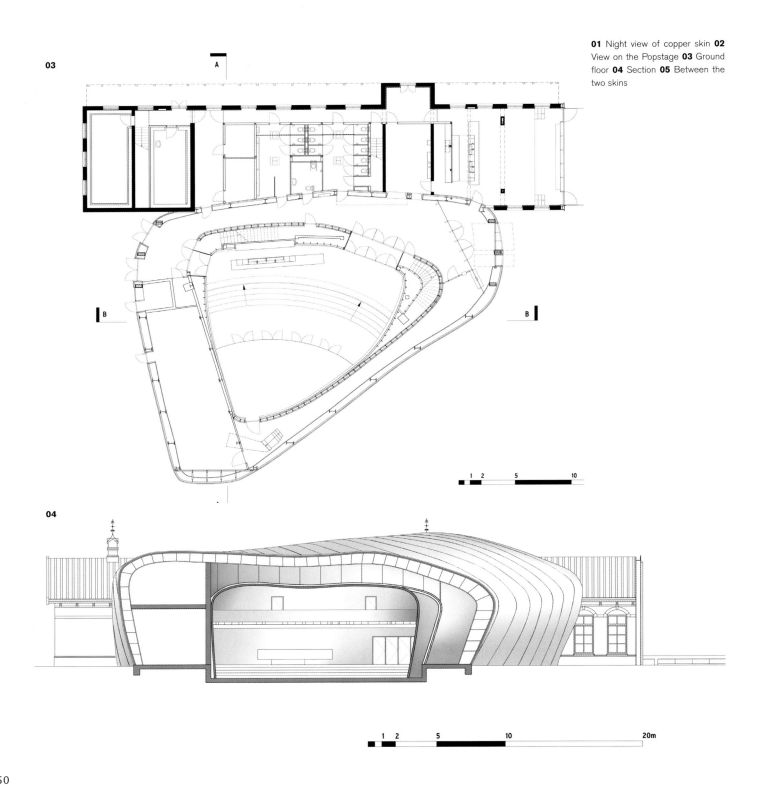

01 Night view of copper skin **02** View on the Popstage **03** Ground floor **04** Section **05** Between the two skins

**Bugatti Company Headquarters,
Château St. Jean, 2004**
Address: 1, Château St. Jean, Dorlisheim, 67120 Molsheim, France. **Gross floor area:** 3,569 m².

Refined manufacturing
ARCHITECTS: Henn Architekten

This is the new workshop of Bugatti Automobiles. It consists of an oval Atelier building that incorporates three testing modules. The oval is 76 metres in length with an overall depth of 45 metres. This is where the assembly of Bugatti cars takes place. Each week one hand-built car is manufactured. The assembly stations are located at the centre of the oval, with the engine subassembly at the western end. The opposite eastern end houses the staff areas on the ground floor and offices on the upper floor. The testing modules for the cars are situated opposite the assembly stations. The modules are connected by transparent walls that allow to view the various testing processes. The testing modules are built of reinforced concrete while the oval – a reminiscence to the Bugatti logo – is a steel structure on a concrete base. The striking façade of the oval is made of perforated metal sheeting.

04

05

06

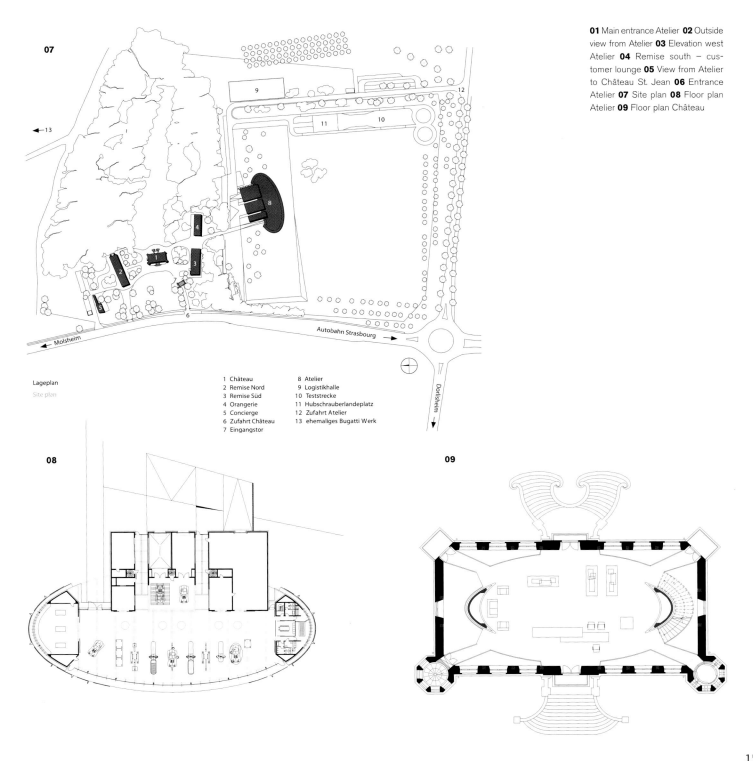

07

← 13

9

12

11   10

8

4

1

3

2

5

6

Molsheim →

Autobahn Strasbourg →

Dorlisheim ↓

Lageplan
Site plan

1 Château
2 Remise Nord
3 Remise Süd
4 Orangerie
5 Concierge
6 Zufahrt Château
7 Eingangstor

8 Atelier
9 Logistikhalle
10 Teststrecke
11 Hubschrauberlandeplatz
12 Zufahrt Atelier
13 ehemaliges Bugatti Werk

08

09

01 Main entrance Atelier **02** Outside view from Atelier **03** Elevation west Atelier **04** Remise south – customer lounge **05** View from Atelier to Château St. Jean **06** Entrance Atelier **07** Site plan **08** Floor plan Atelier **09** Floor plan Château

WKK Energy plant, Utrecht, 2005
Address: Limalaan, De Uithof, Utrecht,
The Netherlands. **Client:** University of Utrecht.
Gross floor area: 950 m².

Skin of steel – a sculptural role
ARCHITECTS: DOK architecten

On an industrial site in Utrecht called De Uithof a new
building was developed to increase the capacity next to
two existing power stations. The size and structure of
the building are largely determined by the technical requirements. The building is completely covered in order
to keep noise pollution to a minimum. The machinery
– giant filters and dampers – are encased within a skin
of steel. The self-supporting steel skin is very striking
and gives the building a sculptural role in the landscape.
The skin is separated from the engine rooms to muffle
the vibrations caused by low frequency sound in the
gas turbines. This gives the building a box-within-a-box
structure. Not an inch of space is wasted. The rigidity of
the covering is achieved by folding the material. Thus,
the form has become the structure, the folds forming
the frame of the building.

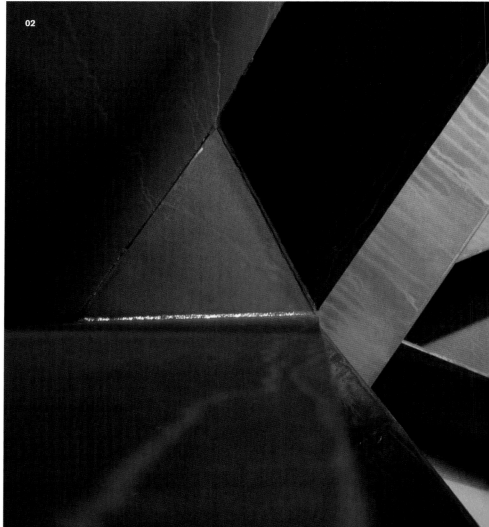

01 Section **02** Corten steel **03** Detail **04** Exterior view

Veranda Parking Garage, Rotterdam, 2005
Address: Siem Heidenstraat 6, 3077 MS Rotterdam, The Netherlands. **Client:** Dienst Stadstoezicht Rotterdam. **Parking spaces underground:** for 330 cars. **Parking spaces above ground:** for 300 cars. **Gross floor area:** 20,000 m². **Ground floor:** 1000 m² shop.

Simplicity and efficiency
ARCHITECTS: Architectenbureau
Paul de Ruiter b.v., Amsterdam

The design of this car park is both simple and efficient. From sloping runways in the middle of the trapezium-shaped floor plan, cars move in a spiral upwards or downwards around the centre. The parking spaces are arranged along the outer walls and next to the central open area and the sloping runway. The façade of the Veranda multi-storey car park is composed of horizontal strips of aluminium, alternated with small strips of mirror glass. To combine plasticity and transparency in the façade, the architect developed the perforated and folded (deep-drawn) aluminium panels. The glass and aluminium panels are contained in extruded aluminium profiles, which were also specially designed for this project. From the inside, the façade acts as a diffuse screen that admits daylight and offers a fragmented view of the outside world. In the evenings, the façade allows artificial light through and the building shines like a huge lantern.

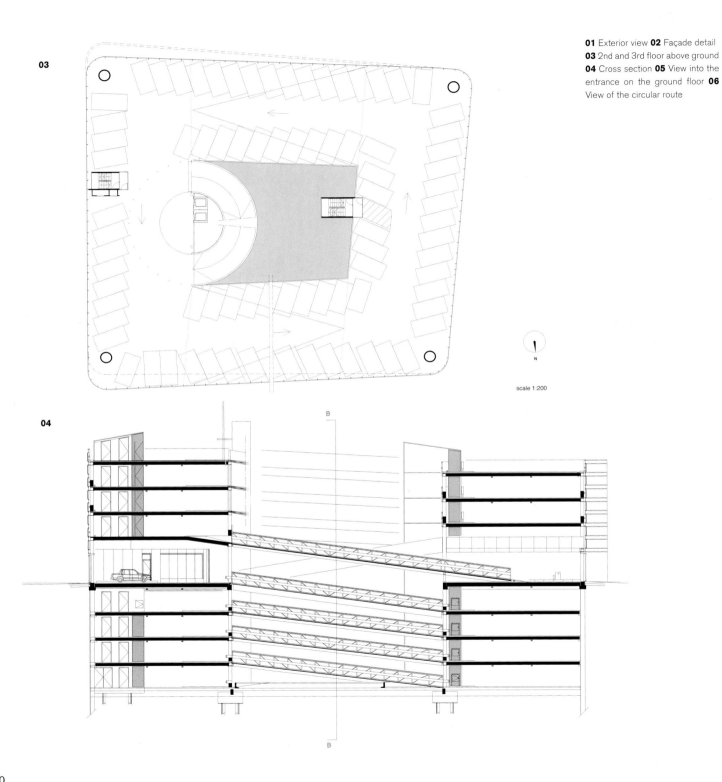

03

04

01 Exterior view **02** Façade detail
03 2nd and 3rd floor above ground
04 Cross section **05** View into the
entrance on the ground floor **06**
View of the circular route

N

scale 1:200

B

B

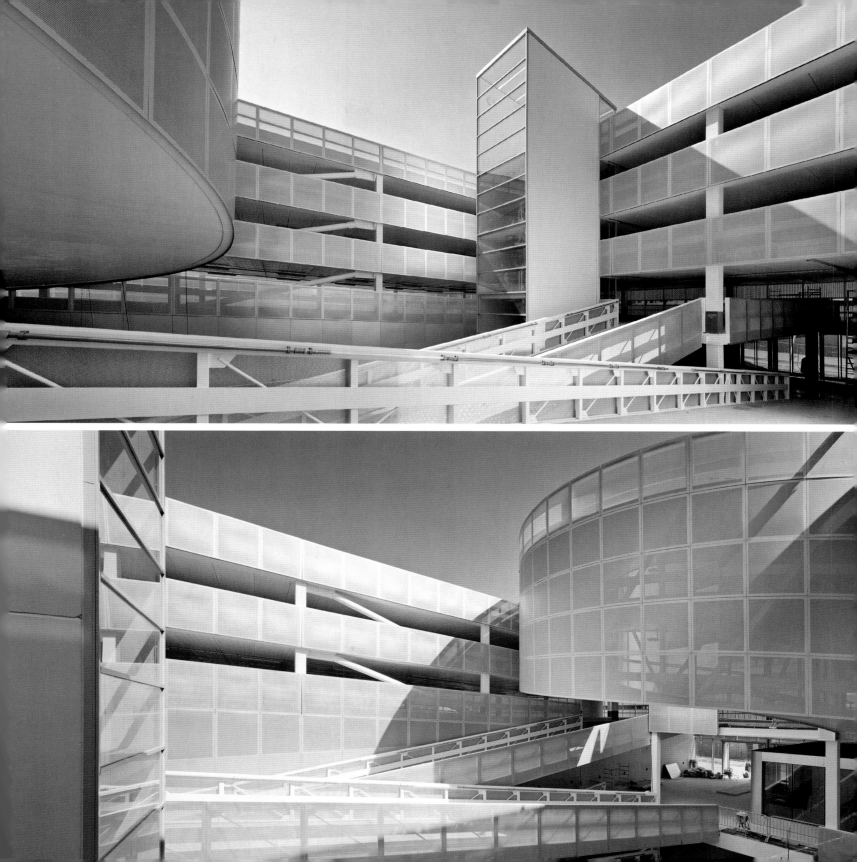

Tea House on Bunker, Vreeland, 2006
Address: Vreeland, The Netherlands. **Gross floor area:** 80 m². **Volume:** 450 m³. **Building site:** 54 m².

Bunker upgrade
ARCHITECTS: Ben van Berkel / UNStudio

This project involves the reprogramming of a historical and derelict building through renovation and addition. The original bunker is part of an intricate water management system that enabled the flooding of land in case of attack. It is situated in a classic Dutch polder landscape. The existing 1936 bunker remains intact except for a portion of the concrete roof where the new structure is connected. The new addition is like an umbrella, an addition that can be removed and does not damage or permanently influence the historic structure. Rather, it appears to have grown out of the still-visible concrete facades of the bunker, jutting out towards the sports fields with its large single window. The space is designed with steel structures within its two main walls that act as floor-to-ceiling beams. These beams are balanced off-centre on two columns that land directly in front of the existing bunker. Stability is achieved by using the massive concrete shell of the bunker as a counterweight, offsetting the forces of the cantilevering extension by connecting it with the two beams.

04

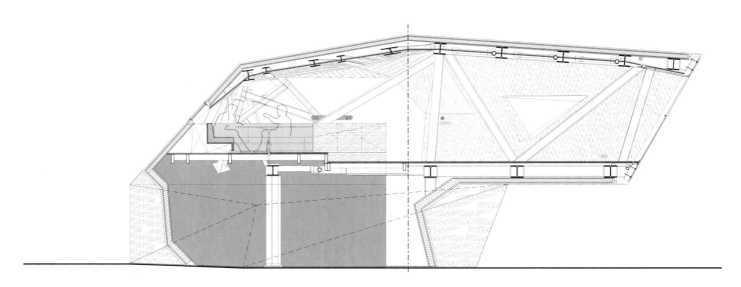

05

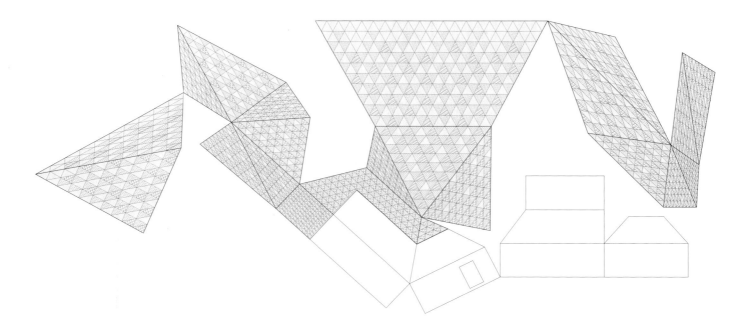

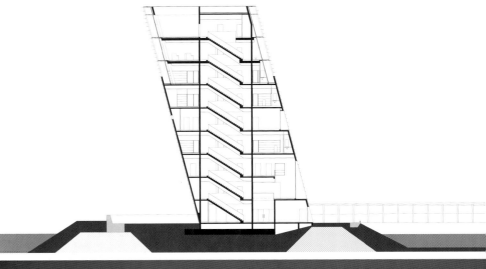

Harbour Control Tower, Lisbon, 2001
Address: Lisbon Port / Pedrouços Dock / Algês, Portugal. **Client:** Administração do Porto de Lisboa – APL. **Gross floor area:** 2,280 m². **Materials:** Load-bearing structure: reinforced concrete; Façade skin: copper sheet in natural finish, bonded to fibre-cement plates and aluminium substructure.

Harbour control
ARCHITECTS: GONÇALO BYRNE,
GB-ARQUITECTOS, Lisbon

The control tower of Lisbon harbour, built to supervise all maritime and fluvial movements in the harbour and along the nearby coast, occupies an exceptional position on the riverfront of old Lisbon. Marking a new starting point to a sequence of historical buildings, and thereby destined to symbolise the old military and commercial control of the harbourfront, the new centre relies more on "invisible" control by electronic media. Repudiating this banalization of the notion of control, the building manifestly assumes the form of a tower. To achieve control, it is essential to dominate, visually and symbolically. In the case of the maritime control centre, this concept was explicitly asked for in the invitation to tender, despite the fact that modern control is a matter of electronic services and visualisation in virtual reality. Metal is a traditional building material in ports. The natural copper plate façade was chosen because copper not only withstands the harsh weather conditions, but also reflects these in its natural ageing process. Each of the façades, depending on the orientation, changes colour differently with time, until eventually all have acquired the same green hue.

01 Longitudinal section **02** Roof terrace **03** North eastern view

02

Wales Millennium Centre, 2004
Address: Bute Place, Cardiff, CF 10 5AL, United Kingdom. **Client:** Wales Millennium Centre Ltd. **Gross floor area:** 37,500 m². **Materials:** stainless steel, stone (slate), timber, concrete and steel structural frame, glazing.

Fundamental qualities
ARCHITECTS: Capita Percy Thomas, Cardiff

The Wales Millennium Centre is a centre for performing arts with a resident community of seven arts organisations, working in dance, choral music, theatre and opera. The centrepiece of the building is the world-class Donald Gordon Theatre, which seats 1,900 people. The theatre is clad in a distinctive metal shell, which projects outwards to define and to shelter the main entrance. The front of the metal shell is distinguished by a unique window in the form of an inscription composed for the building by one of the country's leading poets, Gwyneth Lewis. The metal used in the Wales Millennium Centre was designed to express the fundamental qualities of the material. This means that it is fixed in such a way that its flexibility, ductility and reflectivity are strongly expressed. This acts as a counterpoint to the natural stone cladding. Stainless steel was chosen because of its durability in the maritime setting. The patina was chosen for its variability. It has a strong natural character because – like leaves on a tree – no two steel sheets are exactly alike.

01 Detail of elevation at entrance
02 General view **03** Plan level 0
04 Side elevation of shell **05** Detail
of metal and stone

03

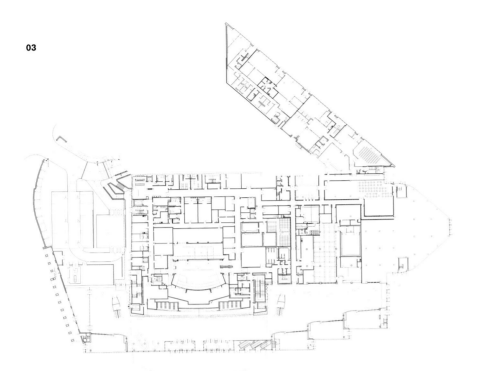

04

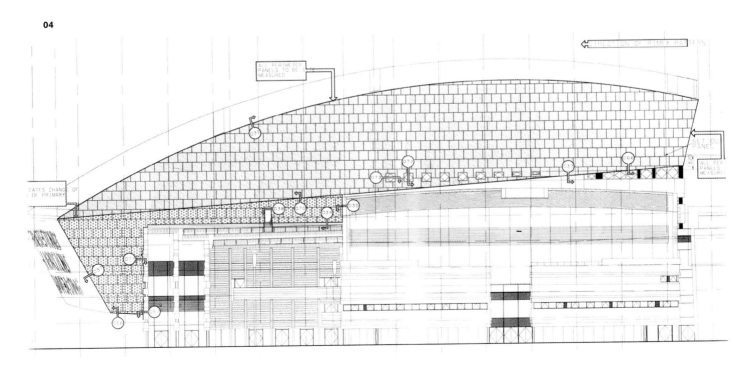

BMW Plant Leipzig – Central Building, 2004
Address: BMW Werk, Leipzig, Germany. **Client:**
BMW AG. **Materials:** self-compacting concrete with
a roof structure assembled using a series of H-steel
beams.

Corporate design

ARCHITECTS: Zaha Hadid with
Patrik Schumacher

In October 2004 BMW moved into the Central Building
at the new Leipzig plant. The building's design facilitates
a radical new interpretation of open office landscape,
providing an even more engaging experience of con-
nectivity and transparency combined with demanding
functionality. The Central Building is the nerve-centre
of the whole factory complex with all the building's activities gathering and branching out again from here.
The knot connects the three main manufacturing departments of Body-in-White, Paint Shop and Assembly
while also serving as the entrance to the plant. The
whole expanse of this side of the factory is oriented and
animated by a force field emanating from the central
building. All movement converging on the site is fun-
nelled through this compression chamber squeezed in
between the three main segments of production. This
planning strategy applies not only to the cycles and tra-
jectories of workers and visitors but also to the production line, which traverses this central point.

01 Cross section through offices **02** Interior view **03** Offices bridge over
the plant's entrance **04** Suspended beltways above offices

Eco-Boulevard of Vallecas, new suburban extension of Madrid, 2007
Address: Bulevar de la Naturaleza, 28053 Madrid, Spain. **Client:** Empresa Municipal de Vivienda y Suelo de Madrid. **Gross floor area:** 22,500 m². **Materials:** steel and recycled materials.

Air-Tree-Art
ARCHITECTS: ecosistema urbano arquitectos
Belinda Tato, José Luis Vallejo,
Diego García-Setién

The proposal for the eco-boulevard in Vallecas can be defined as an urban recycling project with a threefold action plan: to place "air trees" as socially revitalizing elements within an existing urban environment; to densify existing trees; and to reduce and asymmetrically rearrange traffic circulation. Superficial interventions (perforations, fillings, paint, etc.) are also used to reconfigure the existing urban environment. Three pavilions or "air trees" have been designed as open structures to multiply the range of activities that local residents can practice here. Installed in the "non-city" as temporary prostheses, they will be used only until air-conditioned spaces are no longer needed, when the area has been thoroughly regenerated. When that happens these devices should be dismantled, leaving spaces that resemble forest clearings. The "air tree" is a light structure, easily dismantled and self-sufficient in terms of energy: it consumes no more than it can produce by means of photovoltaic panels.

04

05

06

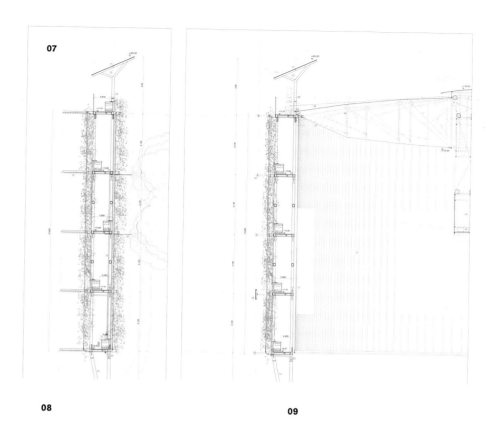

07

08

09

10

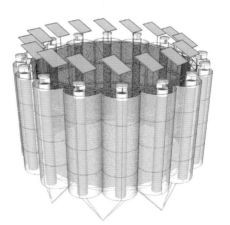

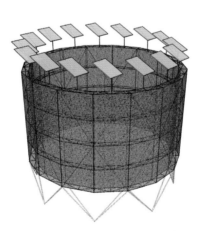

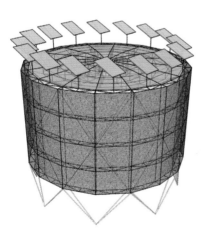

Rooftecture S, 2005
Address: Hyogo Pref., Kobe, Japan. **Client:** Ryosuke and Yasuko Uenishi. **Gross floor area:** 65.7 m². **Materials:** galvanized steel sheet, plywood, wood flooring.

Slopes and architecture
ARCHITECTS: Endo Shuhei Architect Institute

The main theme of this house is the age-old problem of reconciling slopes with architecture. Shuhei's approach involved maximizing the existing features. These were the stone retaining wall at the rear and the improved ground. This approach complemented existing environmental features by creating a balance between the slope and the architecture by adding new elements: an artificial floor supported by a set of five piles and the roof and walls that enclose the space. On the second floor, the roof and floor (the artificial ground that continues on the northern terrace) visually incorporate the stone retaining wall as an inner wall as well as the landscape framed inside the retaining wall and the wall on the western side. The roof/wall was created from a rectangular sheet of metal shingle board. It maintains the logical extensity of the slope and the triangular land form by folding and tilting. States of liberation and closure created though the interaction with the slope define this house's spatial quality.

06

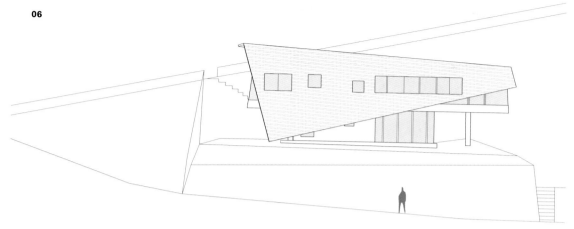

01 View from west 02 Overall view from south 03 Kitchen: looking west 04 Living room: looking east 05 View from west 06 Elevation 07 Plan

07

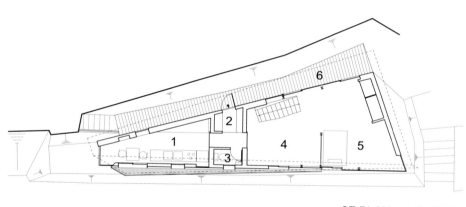

2F PLAN   S=1/200

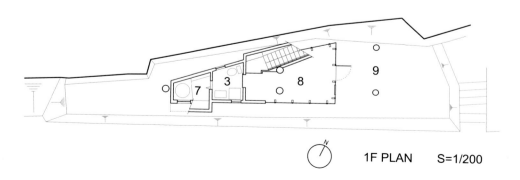

1F PLAN   S=1/200

Echigo-Matsunoyama Museum of Natural Science, 2003
Address: Matsunoyama-machi, Niigata, Japan. **Client:** Matsunayama-machi / Secretariat of Tokamachi Regionwide area Munical cooperation. **Lighting designer:** Masahide Kakudate / Masahide Kakudate Lighting Architect & Associates. **Gross floor area:** 997 m². **Materials:** plasterboard (super-hard board), emulsion paint, fibreglass sheeting, aluminium angles.

Like an Inca ruin
ARCHITECTS:
Takaharu + Yui Tezuka Architects

Located in the mountains of Matsunoyama, a region of Niigata Prefecture known for its heavy winter snowfall, Kyororo is a facility dedicated to educational and research activities in the field of natural science. The facility was built to house both a permanent base for scientists and exhibition spaces for the general public. Great emphasis was placed on incorporating the natural and climatic settings of this environment into the concept. The structure's pitched cross section was inspired by shelters built in the Matsunoyama region to protect local roads from snow. The horizontal plan, shaped like a snake, follows the pattern of the paths surrounding the site. The appearance of the weather-resistant steel outer shell changes with the passage of time. Six months after the Corten plates were welded together on-site, the body was already displaying its characteristic deep brown, striped pattern. From the other side of the valley the building looks like a ruin from the Inca period, its tower seeming to have dominated the tree-tops for ages.

03

04

05

06

01 View of the roof **02** View from the entrance side **03** View from the rear of the building **04** Acrylic window, size 11-by-3.5 metre **05** View of the hall **06** Elevation **07** Plan

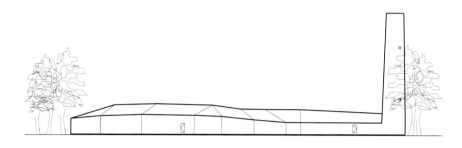

07

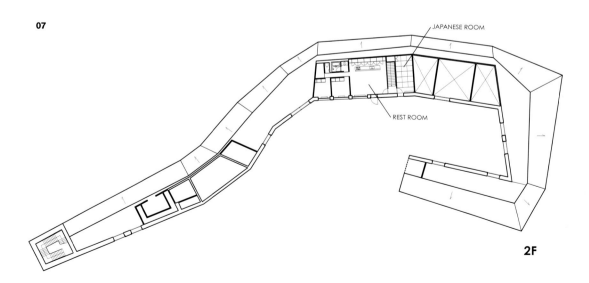

JAPANESE ROOM

REST ROOM

2F

Sachsenhausen Memorial "Station Z", 2005
Address: Straße der Nationen 22, 16515 Oranienburg, Germany.

Artificial and abstract

ARCHITECTS: hg merz architekten museumsgestalter, stuttgart/berlin

An artificial emptiness was created intentionally to lend dignity to the former concentration camp. Symbolism and pathos were avoided by creating an abstract structure. This in turn provides a protective cover and contemplative space that rises above the remains of the former crematorium of "Station Z". The ground plan of the structure takes account of the outline remains of the old buildings but avoids replicating the original dimensions. The shell construction, a steel truss frame, occupies a discreet background position. The primary structure is covered over with a grid, which is spanned externally and internally by a translucent PTFE-coated fibreglass membrane. Its sharp-edged quality is maintained by an artificial vacuum. Presenting a unified appearance both from the outside and the inside, the translucent radiance of this protective structure only becomes apparent when seen in natural light. The use of steel allows the surviving structures to be spanned without using columns.

04

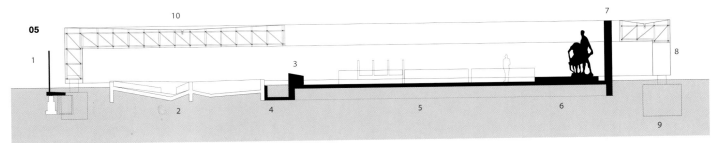

1   Eingang Gedenkstätte

2   Besucherinformationszentrum (BIZ)

3   Lagerstraße

4   Turm A

5   Ehemaliges Häftlingslager

6   Gedenkort »Station Z«

7   Museum Sowjetisches Speziallager

05

1 Ausstellungsfläche auf Glasfaserbetontafeln	6 Sockelplatte für Skulptur
2 Relikte »Station Z«	7 Gedenkwand
3 Ausstellungsfläche »Geschichte der Station Z«	8 Eingang Gedenkort
4 Drainagewanne	9 Brunnengründung Schutzhülle
5 Bodenplatte Gedenkort »Station Z«	10 Schutzhülle

House of Sweden, 2006
Address: Washington D.C., USA. **Responsible architect:** Gert Wingårdh. **Architect in charge:** Gunilla Murnieks. **Client:** National Property Board Sweden. **Total floor area:** approx. 8,150 m², including 1,560 m² garage space.

Facing the Potomac
ARCHITECTS: Gert Wingårdh and Tomas Hansen

This building has seven levels, including a rooftop terrace and underground car park, and was built right up to the property boundary, except at entrance level. This lies at the highest point to which the Potomac River is ever expected to rise. A large flight of steps and a ramp along the entrance side of the building leave the pillars exposed and create a loggia in a classicistic and classically modern style (compare this with Villa Savoie). The entrance floor is the hub of all operations. The part of the building used exclusively for the embassy is on the left together with the reception area. The offices are located on the next floor. The public part of the building has its reception on the right, with a large, glazed exhibition space (the Anna Lind Hall) facing the Potomac River and with a series of multi-purpose exhibition and conference rooms leading off a lower lobby. The top two floors of the building are a residential area with 19 apartments.

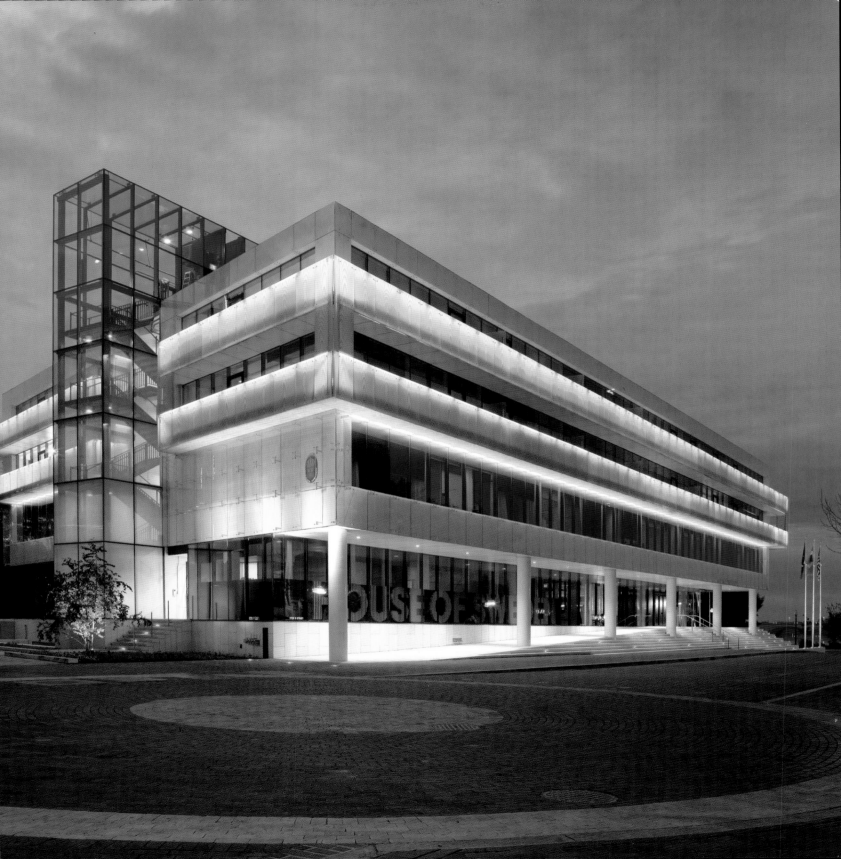

04

05

06

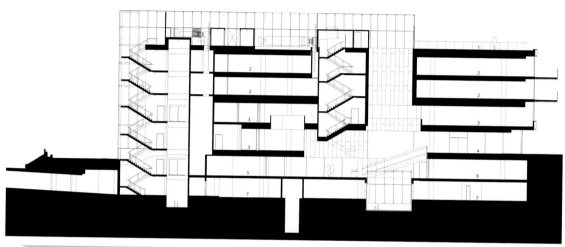

08

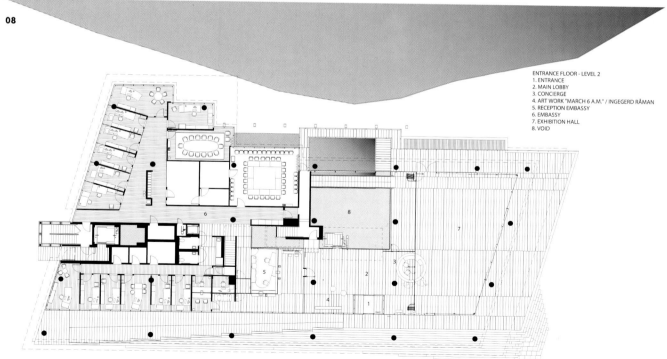

ENTRANCE FLOOR - LEVEL 2
1. ENTRANCE
2. MAIN LOBBY
3. CONCIERGE
4. ART WORK "MARCH 6 A.M." / INGEGERD RÅMAN
5. RECEPTION EMBASSY
6. EMBASSY
7. EXHIBITION HALL
8. VOID

Headquarters of Ferrari S.p.A., Maranello, 2003
Address: Via Abetone Inferiore, 4, Maranello (Modena), Italy. **Client:** Ferrari S.p.A. **Area:** 19,500 m².

Red power
ARCHITECTS: Massimiliano Fuksas, Rome

The building is situated at the centre of the future main entrance to the Ferrari Complex in the town of Maranello. Recently, the complex has been successfully redeveloped. The location of the research centre, between the wind tunnel and the Meccanica Building, emphasises the role of the building and its contribution to the overall image of Ferrari. This building hosts the offices of Ferrari's technical management team. The project tries to accomplish the client's aim of combining a healthy working environment with a strong outward appearance. Between the two main volumes an open space has been created. The water feature within this space is one of the most attractive elements of the building. The building is punctuated by asymmetrical glass boxes that contain the stairs and elevators linking the different levels. The cantilevered main volume creates a dramatic entrance, reinforcing the idea of suspension.

01 Exterior view 02 Open space
03 Glass boxes and stairs 04 Axo-
nometric view 05 Sections 06 View
into the building 07 Interior view

05

Unidade Industrial da Inapal Metal, 2006
Address: Parque Industrial da AutoEuropa, Lote 19,
Quinta do Anjo, Palmela, Portugal. **Client:** Inapal
Metal S.A., Portugal. **Gross floor area:** 12,418 m².

Sensational skin
ARCHITECTS:
Menos é Mais Arquitectos Associados

The Inapal Metal industrial unit is dedicated to the
production of metal components for the automobile
industry and is composed of two apparently autono-
mous volumes. One volume consists of two wings and
a huge cantilever that combine raw material storage
and different sections of production and delivery. The
other consists of two floors where the maintenance
and staff quarters are housed. The design not only
deals with material homogenisation and continuity, but
also embraces a strategy of structural modulation and
constructive rationalization. The focal point of this building is its "skin". A single surface material – trapezoidal
metal cladding – unifies the project. The versatility of
the material in terms of different applications and orientations is explored: revetments sheets are used when a
closed space is required, whereas metal sheeting is cut
in slices and fixed in a honeycomb pattern when it is
necessary to shade, illuminate or ventilate.

01 View from north west of the industrial wings and the cantilever 02 Detail view of the different applications and orientations of the metal cladding 03 General view from south east 04 Sections 05 Interior view of the distribution corridor between the staff and industrial areas 06 Southern view of the space between the staff building and the industrial wing

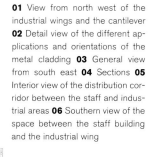

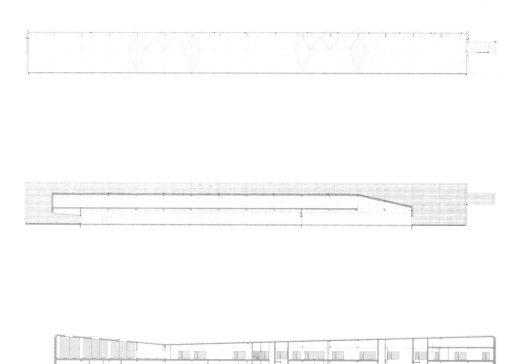

Son-O-House, 2004
Address: 5600 Ekkersrijt, Son en Breugel, The Netherlands. **Client:** Industrieschap Ekkersrijt. **Gross floor area:** 300 m². **Materials:** stainless steel.

A house where sounds live
ARCHITECTS: NOX / Lars Spuybroek

Son-O-House is a typical art project by NOX. It allowed them to proceed more carefully and slowly (over a period of three to four years) while generating a lot of knowledge that they then applied to larger and faster projects. Son-O-House is what one might call "a house where sounds live". It is not a "real" house, but a structure that refers to living and the bodily movements that accompany habit and habitation. In the Son-O-House a sound work continuously generates new sound patterns activated by sensors that pick up the actual movements of visitors. The structure is both an architectural and a sound installation that allows people to not just hear sound in a musical structure, but also to participate in the composition of the sound. It is an instrument, score and studio at the same time. The structure is derived from typical action-landscapes that develop in a house: a fabric of larger scale bodily movements in a corridor or room, together with smaller scale movements around a sink or a drawer.

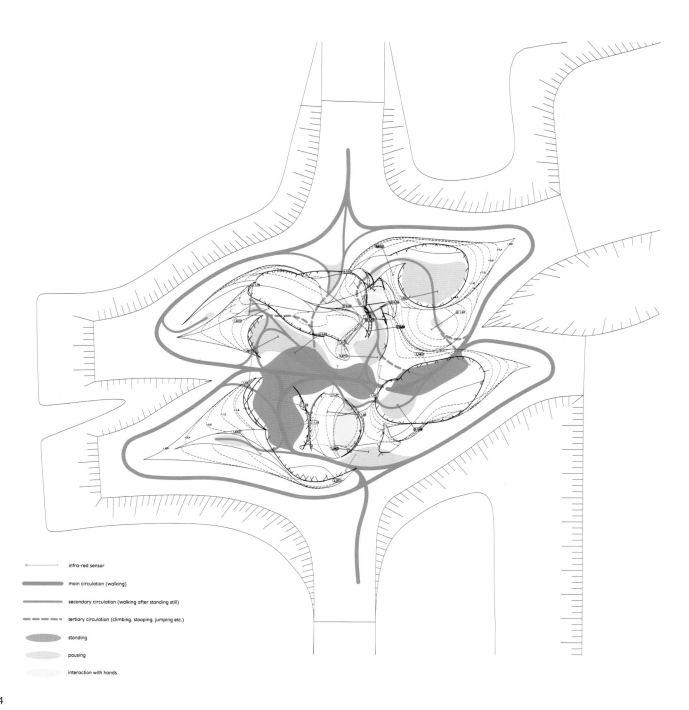

infra-red sensor

main circulation (walking)

secondary circulation (walking after standing still)

tertiary circulation (climbing, stooping, jumping etc.)

standing

pausing

interaction with hands

Project Education Centre: The Core, 2005
Address: Cornwall, United Kingdom. **Landscape architect:** Land Use Consultants. **Acoustic engineer:** Buro Happold. **Client:** Eden Project Limited.

Beauty and proportion

ARCHITECTS: Grimshaw Architects

The Eden Project has been an ongoing project for Nick Grimshaw since its inception in 1996 but received most publicity with the opening of the Biomes in 2001. The Core represents the most important stage in Eden's development since then. The design concept of the Core was developed from naturally occurring geometries, its point of departure being the Fibonacci number series in which the ratio between numbers tends to be 1,618. This sequence appears to underpin our innate understanding of beauty and proportion. The final design was generated from phyllotaxis, which is the mathematical basis for nearly all plant growth; hence the roof structure recalls the arrangement of scales on a pinecone or the seeds in a sunflower head. The concept for the Core is geometrically complex, its structure uses very simple materials and is based on a timber lamella system. The roof is the focal point of the design; its pinecone "scales" are formed by a grid of timber panels, insulated with recycled newspaper. It is clad with a standing-seam system of copper panelling that will weather over time to produce a varied patina. The façade of the building is inclined inwards by ten degrees, which helps assert the significance of the roof structure.

01 Interior view **02** View of the roof
03 Floor plan **04** Section **05** Roof
detail showing pyramid windows

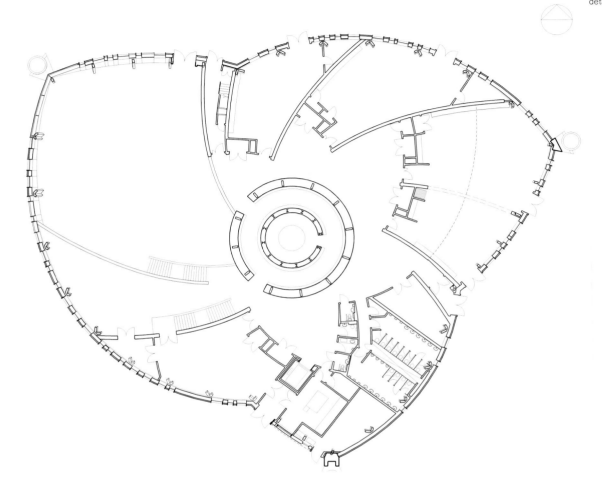

04

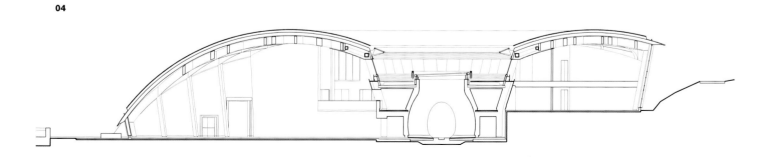

Airbus A380 Manufacturing Halls, 2004
Address: Airbus Manufacturing Plant, Hamburg-Finkenwerder, Germany. **Client:** Airbus Deutschland GmbH. **Gross floor area:** approx. 103,000 m².

High-tech on the Elbe

ARCHITECTS: gmp – Architekten von Gerkan, Marg und Partner
Design: Volkwin Marg with Marc Ziemons,
Partner: Nikolaus Goetze

A column-free steel structure with external main girders spans the 120 x 350 metres major component assembly hall. The façades are articulated by extensive glazing and aluminium cladding and incorporate ribbon windows. Following the completion of the major component assembly hall, the equipment assembly hall was built at the north end of the Hamburg Airbus site. Four column-free assembly stations are located back-to-back here, each measuring 92.5 x 80 metres. Four "tail scoops" on the hall roof provide the required height for work on the aircraft tail. The exterior support structure is a 10-metre-high lattice truss that across the entire length supported by five main columns. Eight transverse truss girders cross the main girder in bend-proof joints and jut out 36 metres from the north façade next to the tail scoops. The 370-metre-long glass façade faces the Elbe river and its slope. By day the glass façade reflects the prevailing sky conditions while in the evening the glare-free interior and exterior lighting creates a glowing light in the hall, and allows the aircraft to be seen from afar.

04

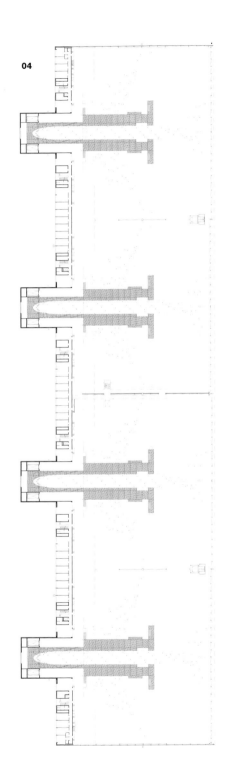

05

06

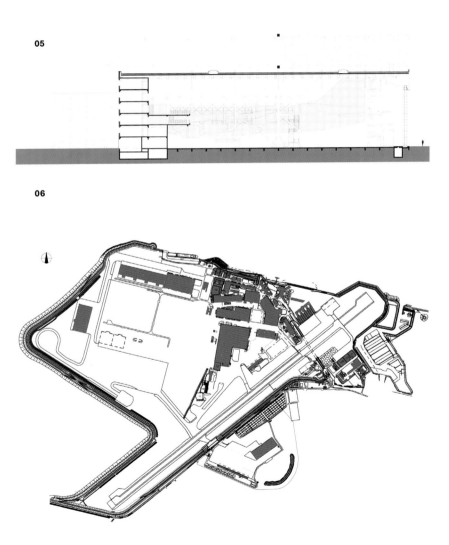

01

DeBrug Headquarters Unilever, 2005
Address: Nassaukade 3, Rotterdam, The Netherlands.
Urban design: West 8 Urban Design & Landscape
Architecture. **Interior design:** New Creations.
Client: Dura Vermeer Vastgoed BV. **Tenant:**
Unilever Nederland B.V. **Gross floor area:** 15,000 m².
Materials: metal, concrete, glass, aluminium.

Bridge building
ARCHITECTS: JHK Architecten

This project began with a request for a characteristic, daringly designed office building linked to Unilever Nederland's factory site on the Nassaukade street. In addition to being a distinctive concept office building, the structure was also intended to be part of a new urban fabric, in size and scale considerably smaller than a typical 14,000 m² office building. Dura Vermeer, West 8 Urban Design and JHK Architecten teamed up and came up with a daring plan. Rather than using the originally intended Oranjeboom location, they decided to build the company headquarters on top of the existing factory. This prominent "bridge building" would then blend in with the surrounding bridges and harbour architecture. The offices, which were prefabricated next to the factory, offer a breathtaking, panoramic view of the city centre on the other side of the Maas river. Atriums and patios allow light to enter the building. Open spaces are strategically located to ensure adequate illumination in the central zone.

02

04

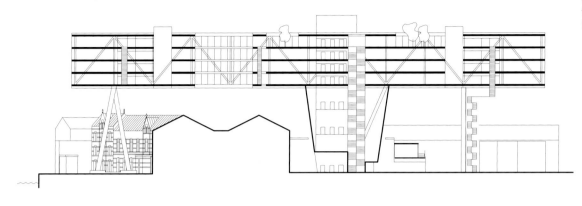

05

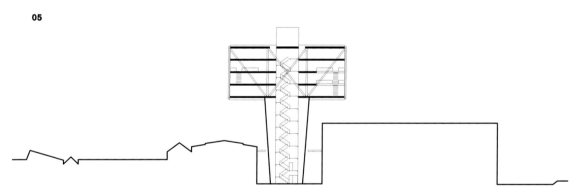

06

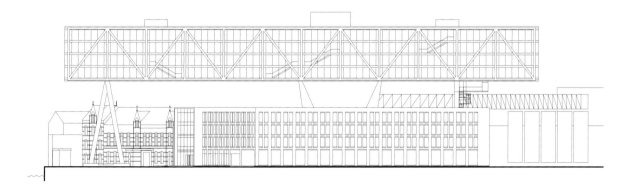

01 Office by night **02** New skyline Rotterdam **03** Office above the existing factory **04–06** Sections and façade **07** View through central void **08** View of the skyline of Rotterdam

"Culture Island" in Middelfart, 2005
Address: Middelfart, Denmark. **Client:** Middelfart Municipality. **Gross floor area:** 4,500 m². **Engineer:** Hundsbæk & Henriksen.

Sculptural landmark in the harbourscape

ARCHITECTS: schmidt hammer lassen

The "Culture Island" in Middelfart is a gleaming, distinctive presence on the newly created island off the Middelfart waterfront. The circle described by the island and marina contrasts with the rectangularity of the landward side. The building's dynamic form responds to the uniqueness of its location on the waterfront. The arts and community complex has extensive glazed sections and opens up towards the water while the vertically slit, zinc façades enclose the interior spaces, creating tranquillity and intimacy. A cleft splits the complex into two: a double-height foyer space lit from above with a roof light that affords a glimpse of the sky. On one side is the library, and on the other the tourist information office, a cinema and restaurant. Both sides command views across the Little Belt sea. The arts and community centre's trapezoidal forms and curvilinear surfaces are an interpretation of the sea and sails. Seen from the surrounding area, bridges and boats, the complex appears as a sculptural landmark in the harbourscape.

01 Exterior view **02** Plan **03** Glass and zinc façade

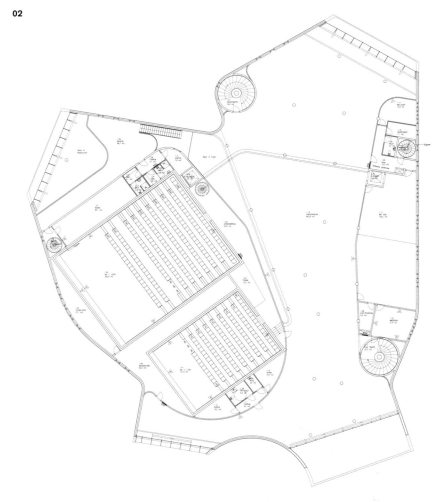

City Hall, Graz, 2002
Address: Messeplatz 1, 8010 Graz, Austria. **Client:** Municipality of Graz, Building Authority. **Gross floor area:** approx. 28,600 m².

Four powerful columns
ARCHITECTS: Klaus Kada

Four massive columns support the 150 x 70 metre roof, creating space for 11,000 visitors in the hall itself. The concept of a flexible continuous space under one roof is achieved by means of 18-metre-high moveable walls and doors across the whole rear area of the hall. As a result the hall can be opened out onto the green parkland on the east side, turning the interior and exterior spaces into a single flexible integrated unit. A tower rises above this impressive building and provides offices on the first four floors for event organisers and other institutions.

05

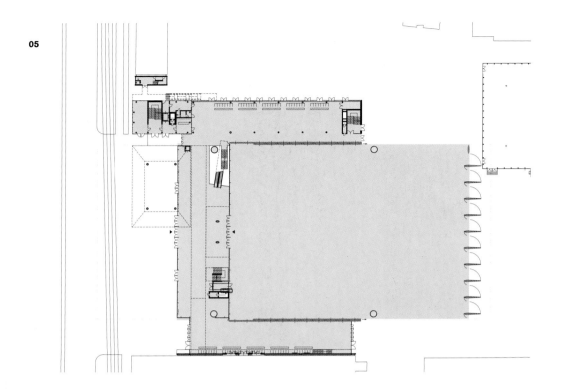

06

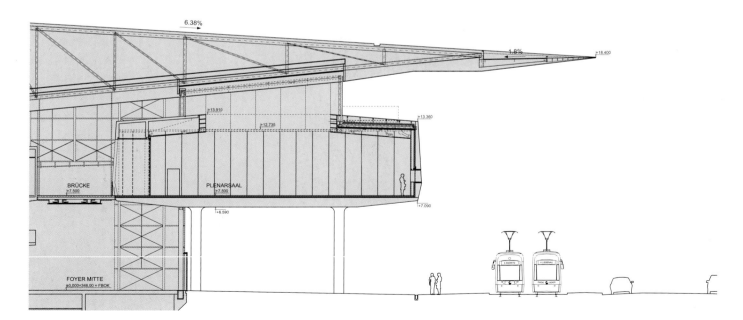

6.38%

1.8%

+18.400

+13.910

+13.360

+12.735

BRÜCKE
+7.500

PLENARSAAL
+7.500

+6.590

+7.090

FOYER MITTE
±0,000=346,00 = FBOK

01

Paul Klee Centre, 2005
Address: Berne, Switzerland. **Consultants:** Ove Arup &
Partners, B+S Ingenieure AG. **Client:** Maurice E. and
Martha Müller Foundation.

02

Three hills
ARCHITECTS: Renzo Piano Building Workshop
in collaboration with arb, Berne

Renzo Piano has built a museum with adjoining rooms
that feature powerful, free-spanning steel arches sug-
gestive of a long dead animal or ship run aground. The
"ribs" are gradually overgrown and concealed, the house
or ship blending in with the landscape. This affords a
view of the roofs, allowing one to see how their outer
skins are made up of various layers, how steel girders
with a combined length of almost 4 kilometres mould
them into a large variety of shapes and curves, and
how the lattice structures are submerged in sand and
finally overgrown with grass. The three "hills" under the
arches are connected by a gently curving museum road
that follows the curve of the passing motorway. The
three hills are not situated parallel, but sympathetically
angled in relation to one another. The segments of
the 64-metre free-spanning beams are never the
same and vary between 1.2 m in the valleys and 80 cm
at the peaks.

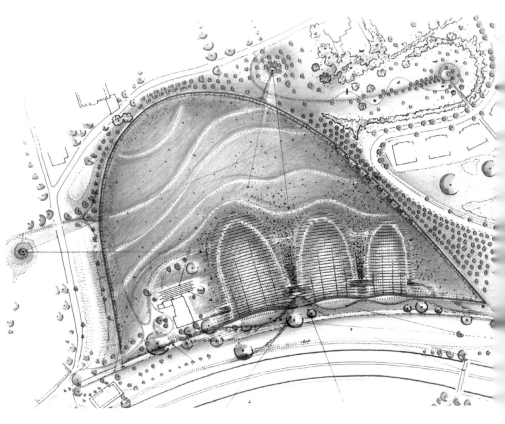

01 Rear view of the museum **02** Site plan **03** Detail of the structure

New Trade Fair Milan, 2005
Total floor area: 2,000,000 m². **Building area:** 1,000,000 m². **Exhibition area:** more than 400,000 m². **Congress centre:** 47,000 m².

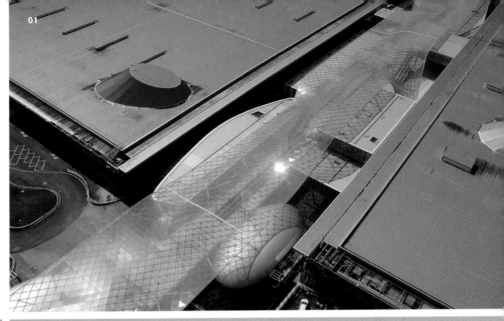

"Contaminated" art

ARCHITECTS: Massimiliano Fuksas, Rome

The New Trade Fair is an important project for the Milan region. Judged by its dimensions it is one of the largest buildings in Europe. It is part of a wider structure of suburban space located on the outskirts of the city. This space wants to become "geography" – it wants to be "landscape". The project is characterized by a central axis. The transparent covering of the axis modifies space and represents a vision of continuity. Service centre, offices and exhibition areas are scattered within the vast site area. The pavilions are situated on both sides of the axis. The steel panel façades reflect images of people walking. The main entrances to the complex are sculpturally designed as the two ends of a path. The architecture can be described as "contaminated" art; it survives by relaying other "universes", it controls movement and changes, it tries to represent what is going on. Architecture is not only inspired by other architecture, but also relates directly to people. In a climate that generally produces very few visions of the future, this project creates dynamic scenarios. Clearly there is still a demand for architecture, a demand for emotion.

04

05

06

07

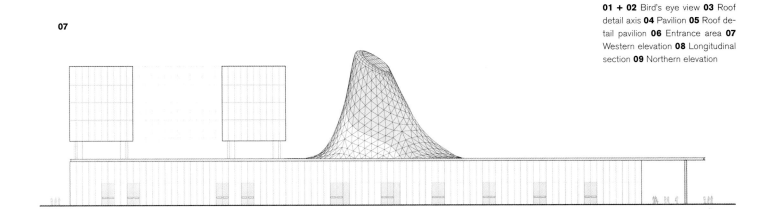

08

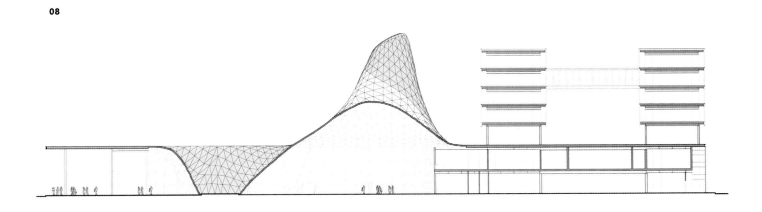

09

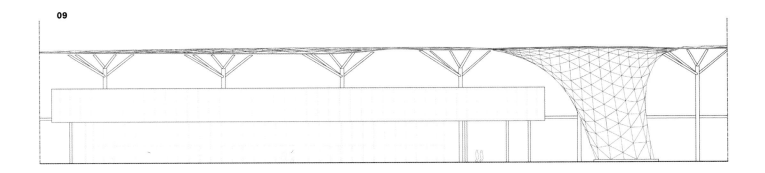

BMW Project House in the Research and Innovation Centre Munich, 2004
Address: BMW, 80788 Munich, Germany.
Client: BMW AG, Munich. **Gross floor area:** 88,500 m².

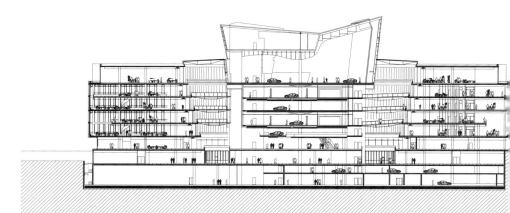

Enjoying research
ARCHITECTS: Henn Architekten

A new type of collaborative product development process has been made possible by a new way of organising space in the Project House of the Research and Innovation Centre at BMW AG Munich. The studio workshop is situated as a "building within a building" in the central atrium of the 100 x 100 metres edifice. The different stages of each project are presented on separate levels using real models in a rapid prototyping process. These levels are directly visible from the surrounding project areas. Two new forms of communication are facilitated by this layout: each developer can switch between virtual work on a computer screen and the real model. By spatially centring the actual product, a visual focal point is created that brings together the right people (collective intelligence) at the right time (real-time).

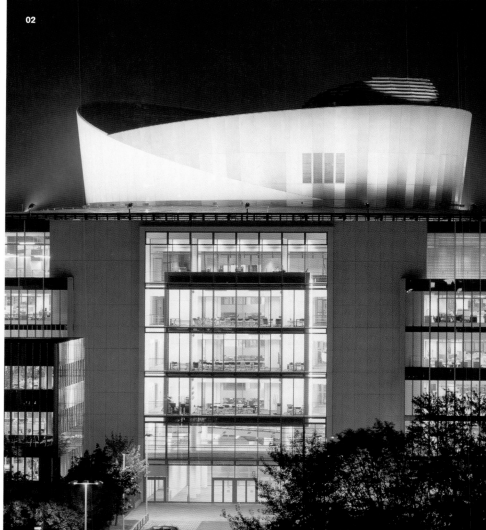

01 Longitudinal section **02** Interface element showing presentation studio on the 5th floor **03** View through roof skylight into the atrium void

Centre for Modern Music / BIMhuis, 2005
Address: Piet Hein Kade 1, Amsterdam, The Netherlands. **Client:** Amsterdam Municipality. **Gross floor
area:** 18,000 m². **Materials:** steel structural columns.

A floating roof
ARCHITECTS: 3XN Architects, Copenhagen

The new Centre for Modern Music / BIMhuis in Amsterdam is all about music. It brings together two well
established cultural institutions, the Ijsbreker centre for
modern music and the BIMhuis for jazz and improvised
music, at a new common location. The prominent pier-
head location faces the Ij river yet is still closely connected to the inner canal city. The Muziekgebouw (its
Dutch name) consists of a "plinth" with a huge set of
stairs with the BIMhuis hovering over the plinth and the
slanted heavy form of the Ijsbreker cutting into the stairs.
Seen from a distance the Muziekgebouw has the weight
of an urban landmark yet up close the scheme dissolves
into individual elements. The high degree of exposure
was intensely considered. The building has five almost
equally weighted façades, including two that face the Ij
and one facing the city and the future Zouthaven water
basin. Transparency between interior and exterior was
essential in the Muziekgebouw. The large glass façade
is therefore supported by slender steel columns that
minimize matter, as only steel can do.

03

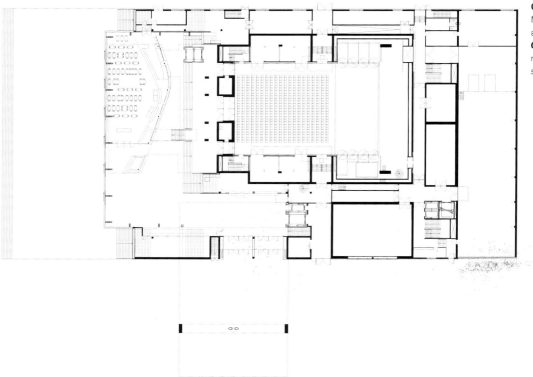

01 Foyer decks expand into the open public space **02** Slender steel structure in the large glass façade **03** Level 01 **04** Section **05** The "gorge" between the Muziekgebouw concert hall (right) and the BIMhuis concert hall (left) **06** Glass façade supported by minimal steel lattice girders to ensure maximum transparency

04

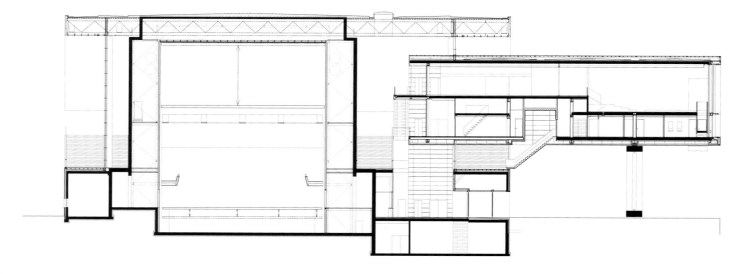

Walt Disney Concert Hall, Los Angeles, 2003
Address: 135 North Grand Avenue, 90012 Los Angeles, California, USA. **Client:** Los Angeles Philharmonic.
Gross floor area: 18,580 m².

Typical Gehry
ARCHITECTS: Frank O. Gehry

The focus of the design is the 2,265-seat main concert hall, whose interior and form are a direct expression of acoustic parameters. Seating surrounds the orchestra platform. The wooden walls and the sail-like wooden ceiling forms give one the impression of being within a great ship. A pipe organ designed in conjunction with the interior occupies a central position between the seating blocks at stage rear. Skylights and a large window at the rear of the hall allow natural light to enhance daytime concerts. The exterior of the concert hall is clad in stainless steel panels. The building's orientation, combined with the curving and folding exterior walls, present highly sculptural compositions as viewers move along adjacent paths and through the surrounding gardens and plazas. An extensive backstage technical area surrounds the concert hall and opens onto a private garden for musicians.

03

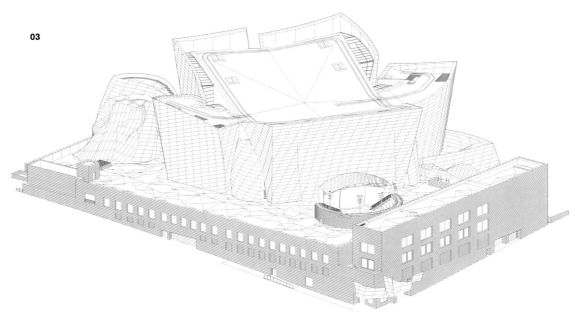

01 Entrance area of the concert hall **02** Exterior view **03** Perspective **04** Plans **05** Night view

04

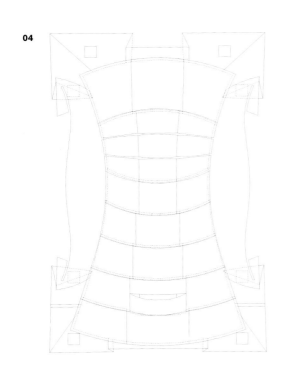
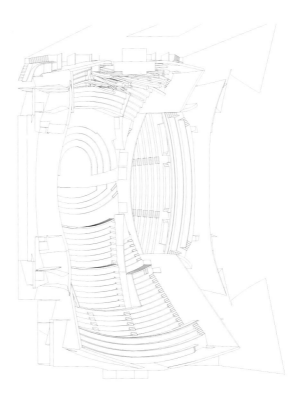

240

Padre Pio Pilgrimage Church, 2004
Address: S. Giovanni Rotondo (Foggia), Italy. **Client:** Provincia dei Frati Minori Cappuccini di Foggia.

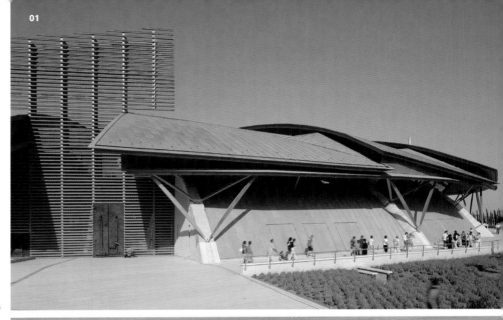

Pilgrimage destination for architects

ARCHITECTS: Renzo Piano Building Workshop

This church is intended to serve the growing number of pilgrims flocking to visit the place where Padre Pio, the Capuchin monk famous for his stigmata, used to live. The challenge presented by the project lies in the use of local stone as a structural material. San Giovanni Rotondo is one of the most-visited pilgrimage destinations in Italy. Every year, hundreds of thousands of pilgrims gather there to pay homage to the memory of Padre Pio. To accommodate the ever-increasing number of followers, the monks decided to build a larger place of worship. The project involved building a larger church, not far from the site where the existing church and monastery are located. The dome is supported by about twenty two arches, made of local limestone. The largest internal arch is 16 metres high and 50 metres long. What was the principal structural element in Gothic cathedrals has here been subjected to new experiments using cutting-edge technology (computerized structural designs, laser-based cross sectional images, etc.).

242

04

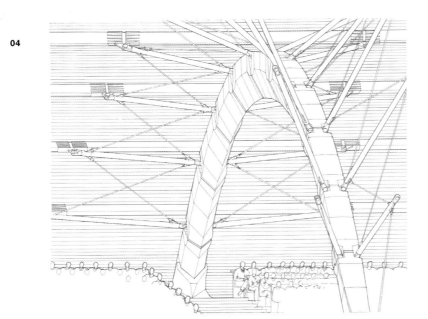

01 West face with slatted brise-soleil **02** Detail of the roof structure made of pre-oxided copper **03** Church square paved with Apricena stone **04** Sketch of one of the arches supporting the roof **05** Site plan **06** Interior view, showing the arches' structure **07** Detail of external arches

05

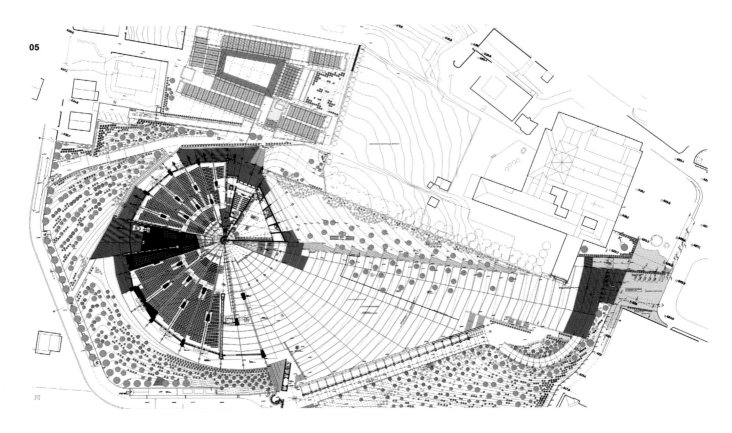

Bianimale Nomadic Museum, 2005
Address: Pier 54, New York City, USA. **Gross floor area:** 4,180 m². **Materials:** containers, paper tubes, vinyl chloride sheeting.

Chessboard pattern

ARCHITECTS: Shigeru Ban Architects

The Nomadic Museum was an almost 4,200 square metre temporary structure housing "Ashes and Snow", an exhibition of large-scale photographic works by artist Gregory Colbert that was on view from March 5 to June 6, 2005. The 20-by-205-metre-long museum was constructed on an historic waterfront pier. It is architect Shigeru Ban's first building in New York and the city's first public building constructed of shipping containers. The structure, which was disassembled and reconstructed as "Ashes and Snow" travelled, provided a transitory environment that evokes the journey of the exhibition and physically frames the artist's work within the context of conservation. The 2.5-by-2.6-metre-high containers were stacked in a checkerboard pattern 10.5 metres high to form the walls of the museum. The openings between the containers were filled with sloping fabric-like membranes. The containers are rented und used temporarily at every place of the exhibition. This exhibition moved to Santa Monica in 2006 and to Tokyo in 2007.

01 Interior view **02** View of the historic waterfront pier **03** Isometric perspective **04** Floor plan **05** Exterior view

03

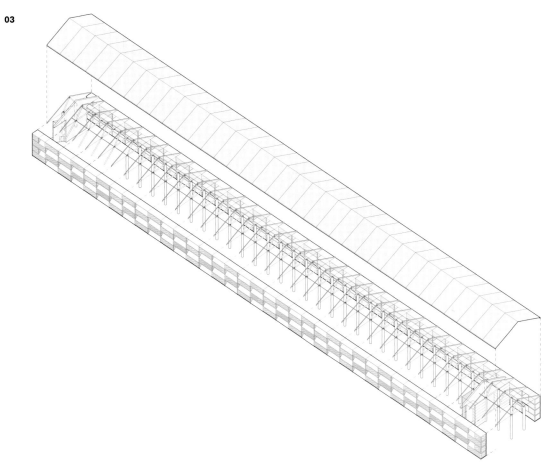

04

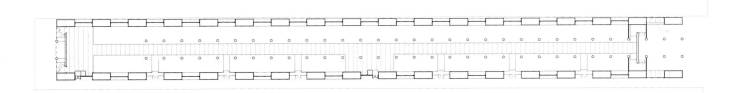

RCHITECTS

INDEX

123

3XN Architects → 58, 234
Strandgade 98
1401 Copenhagen K (Denmark)
T +45.8731.4848
F +45.7026.2649
webmaster@3xn.dk
www.3xn.dk

A

Allmann Sattler Wappner Architekten
→ 82
Nymphenburger Straße 125
80636 Munich (Germany)
T +49.89.13.99.25.0
F +49.89.13.99.25.99
info@allmannsattlerwappner.de
www.allmannsattlerwappner.de

SMC ALSOP → 132
Parkgate Studio
41 Parkgate Road
London SW11 4NP (United Kingdom)
T +44.20.7978.7878
office@smcalsop.com
www.smcalsop.com

arb Arbeitsgruppe → 226
Brunnadernstraße 28b
3006 Berne (Switzerland)
T +41.31.3516002
F +41.31.3511403
arb@arb.ch
www.arb.ch

Augustin und Frank Architekten → 116
Schlesische Straße 29–30
10997 Berlin (Germany)
T +49.30.612843.57
F +49.30.612843.59
augustin_und_frank@t-online.de
www.augustinundfrank.de

B

Shigeru Ban Architects → 246
5-2-4 Matsubara Setagaya-ku
Tokyo (Japan)
T +81.3.3324.6760
F +81.3.3324.6789
tokyo@shigerubanarchitects.com
www.shigerubanarchitects.com

Barkow Leibinger Architekten → 94
Schillerstraße 94
10625 Berlin (Germany)
T +49.30.315712.0
F +49.30.315712.29
info@barkowleibinger.com
www.barkowleibinger.com

Baumschlager-Eberle
Ziviltechniker GmbH
→ 100
Lindauer Straße 31
6911 Lochau (Austria)
T +43.5574.43079.0
F +43.5574.43079.30
office@baumschlager-eberle.com
www.baumschlager-eberle.com

Reiner Becker → 120
Hebbelstraße 39
14469 Potsdam (Germany)
T +49.331.23329.0
F +49.331.23329.79
info@architekturbuero-becker.de
www.architekturbuero-becker.de

blank studio → 136
Joao Moura, 1175 – Pinheiros
Sao Paulo (Brazil)
T +55.11.3088.7223
info@blankstudio.com.br

GONÇALO BYRNE
GB-ARQUITECTOS → 166
Rua da Escola Politécnica 285
1250-101 Lisbon (Portugal)
T +351.213.804.190
F +351.213.804.199
geral@byrnearq.com
www.byrnearq.com

C

Capita Percy Thomas → 168
Eastgate House
35–43 Newport Road
Cardiff CF24 0SB (United Kingdom)
T +44.2920.224334
F +44.2920.383854
www.capitapercythomas.co.uk

D

Deadline → 90
Britta Jürgens, Matthew Griffin
Hessische Straße 5
10115 Berlin (Germany)
T +49.30.285.999.34
F +49.30.285.999.36
post@deadline.de
www.deadline.de

Michel Desvigne → 20

DOK architecten → 156
Entrepotdok 86
1001 ME Amsterdam (The Netherlands)
T +31.20.34497.00
F +31.20.34497.99
post@dokarchitecten.nl
www.dokarchitecten.nl

Döring Dahmen Joeressen Architekten → 64
Hansaallee 321
40549 Düsseldorf (Germany)
T +49.211.537553.0
F +49.211.537553.75
info@ddj.de
ww.ddj.de

Dominik Dreiner Architekt → 26
Wiesenweg 21
76571 Gaggenau (Germany)
T +49.7225.98.26.0
F +49.7225.98.26.20
mail@dominikdreiner.de
www.dominikdreiner.de

Frédéric Druot → 20

L

Léon Wohlhage Wernik Architekten → 10
Leibnizstraße 65
10629 Berlin (Germany)
T +49.30.327.600.0
F +49.30.327.600.60
post@leonwohlhagewernik.de
www.leonwohlhagewernik.de

LMN Architects → 56
801 Second Avenue, Suite 501
Seattle, WA 98104 (USA)
T +1.206.682.3460
F +1.206.343.9388
design@lmnarchitects.com
www.lmnarchitects.com

M

m2r-architecture → 42
2 Spitfire Studios
63–71 Collier Street
London N1 9BE (United Kingdom)
T +44.20.7837.4545
F +44.20.7837.4555
london@m2r.eu
www.m2r-architecture.com

m3xh . Jörg Baumeister → 114
Rebenring 33
38106 Braunschweig (Germany)
T +49.531.3804.160
F +49.531.3804.169
baumeister@m3xh.de
www.m3xh.de

Menos é Mais Arquitectos Associados
→ 198
rua S. Francisco, n°5, 3° andar
4050-548 Porto (Portugal)
T +351.22.201.0451
F +351.22.201.0451
www.menosemais.com

hg merz architekten museumsgestalter
→ 186
Schwedter Straße 34a
10435 Berlin (Germany)
T +49.30.278777.0
F +49.30.278777.50
berlin@hgmerz.com

Ostendstraße 110
70188 Stuttgart (Germany)
T +49.711.707128.24
F +49.711.707128.60
stuttgart@hgmerz.com
www.hgmerz.com

Murray Ó Laoire Architects → 78
3 Victoria Road
Cork (Ireland)
T +353.21.496.7777
F +353.21.492.4800
cork@murrayolaoire.com
www.murrayolaoire.com

N

Anna B. Nicolas → 16
Jungfrauenthal 8
20149 Hamburg (Germany)
T +49.40.463919

NOX / Lars Spuybroek → 202
Conradstraat 38 / Postbus 620
3000 AP Rotterdam (The Netherlands)
T +31.10.4772853
F +31.10.4772853
info@noxarch.com
www.noxarch.com

O

O.M. Architekten BDA
Rainer Ottinger, Thomas Möhlendick
→ 108
Kaffeetwete 3
38100 Braunschweig (Germany)
T +49.531.261593.0
F +49.531.261593.1
info@omarchitekten.de
www.omarchitekten.de

OMA → 56
Heer Bokelweg 149
3032 AD Rotterdam (The Netherlands)
T +31.10.243.82.00
F +31.10.243.82.02
office@oma.nl
www.oma.nl

ONL [Oosterhuis_Lénárd] → 86
Essensburgingel 94c
3022 EG Rotterdam (The Netherlands)
T +31.10.2447039
F +31.10.2447041
info@oosterhuis.nl
www.oosterhuis.nl

P

Périphériques architects
Emmanuelle Marin, Anne-Françoise Jumeau
and David Trottin → 34
4, passage de la Fonderie
75011 Paris (France)
T +33.1.4355.5995
F +33.1.4355.6484
agences@peripheriques-architectes.com
www.peripheriques-architectes.com

Renzo Piano Building Workshop → 226, 242
Via Rubens 29
16158 Genoa (Italy)
T +39.010617.11
F +39.010617.1350
italy@rpbw.com
www.rpbw.com

André Poitiers Architekt RIBA Stadtplaner
→ 74
Großer Burstah 36–38
22083 Hamburg (Germany)
T +49.40.375198.08.9
F +49.40.375198.21

PSP Architekten Ingenieure → 14
Goldbekplatz 2
22303 Hamburg (Germany)
T +49.40.278489.0
F +49.40.278489.59
mail@arch-psp-hamburg.de
www.architekten-psp.de

R

CARSTEN ROTH ARCHITEKT → 124
Rentzelstraße 10b
20146 Hamburg (Germany)
T +49.40.41170.30
F +49.40.41170.330
info@carstenroth.com
www.carstenroth.com

Architectenbureau Paul de Ruiter b.v.
→ 158
Leidestraat 8–10
1017 PA Amsterdam (The Netherlands)
T +31.20.626.3244
F +31.20.623.7002
info@paulderuiter.nl
www.paulderuiter.nl

S

Philippe SAMYN and PARTNERS → 24
1537, Chaussee de Waterloo
1180 Brussels (Belgium)
T +32.23749060
F +32.23747550
sai@samynandpartners.be
www.samynandpartners.be

schmidt hammer lassen → 220
Aaboulevarden 37
Clemensborg PO Box 5117
8000 Aarhus (Denmark)
T +45.86201900
F +45.86184513
info@shl.dk
www.shl.dk

she_architekten → 16
Pilatuspool 7a
29355 Hamburg (Germany)
T +49.40.28809804
F +49.40.28809806
office@she-arch.com
www.she-arch.com

Endo Shuhei Architect Institute → 178
Domus AOI 5F 5-15-11 Nishetema
Kita-ku Osaka
530-0047 Osaka (Japan)
T +81.6.6312.7455
T +81.6.6312.7456
endo@paramodern.com
www.paramodern.com

Francis Soler → 20
27 rue du Cherche Midi
75006 Paris (France)
T +33.142224046
F +33.142221250
courriel@soler.fr
www.soler.fr

**sskprojektgemeinschaft
Straub – Schneider – Kern
Dipl.-Ing. Architekten** → 30
Fafnerstraße 24
80639 Munich (Germany)
T +49.89.54645706
F +49.89.54645740
info@ssk-p.de
www.ssk-p.de

T

Takaharu + Yui Tezuka Architects → 182
1-19-9-3F Todoroki Setagayaku
158-0082 Tokyo (Japan)
T +81.3.3703.7056
F +81.3.3703.7038
tez@sepia.ocn.ne.jp
www.tezuka-arch.com

Architektenteam THS/PASD → 48
Feldmeier _ Wrede
Elberfelder Sraße 32
58095 Hagen (Germany)
T +49.2331.12395.0
F +49.2331.182617
info@pasd.de
www.pasd.de

**THÜS FARNSCHLÄDER
ARCHITEKTEN** → 104
Schulterblatt 124
20357 Hamburg (Germany)
T +49.40.491.10.11
F +49.40.493.231
office@tfarchitekten.de
www.tfarchitekten.de

U

Ben van Berkel / UNStudio → 162
Stadhouderskade 113
1073 AX Amsterdam (The Netherlands)
T +31.20.57020.40
F +31.20.57020.41
info@unstudio.com
www.unstudio.com

V

Ver.de Landschaftsarchitektur GbR → 30
Ganzenmüllerstraße 7
85354 Freising (Germany)
T +49.8161.140.993
F +49.8161.140.996
info@gruppe-ver.de
www.gruppe-ver.de

W

Weber Hofer Partner AG → 68
Zimmerlistraße 6
8040 Zurich (Switzerland)
T +41.44.4969555
F +41.44.4969560
weber-hofer@swissonline.ch

Wingårdh Arkitektkontor AB → 190
Kungsgatan 10 A
411 19 Göteborg (Sweden)
T +46.31.743.7000
F +46.31.711.9838
wingardhs@wingardhs.se
www.wingardhs.se

Z

Zwarts & Jansma Architects → 46
Postbus 2129 Oosterdokskade 5
1000 CC Amsterdam (The Netherlands)
T +31.20.535.22.00
F +31.20.535.22.11
info@zja.nl
www.zwarts.jansma.nl

Picture Credits

Aldershoff, Roos, Amsterdam 216 r. a., 217
Archivio Fuksas, Rome 228 r., 229, 230
Arens, Uwe, Berlin 120 l.
Auckland, Craig, Bristol 169, 171
Bennett, Valerie, London 162 l.
Berengo Gardin, Gianni, Milan 242 r. b.
Bergs, Tamara, Berlin 120 r.
Boegly, Luc, Paris 34–36
Bormann, Andreas, Braunschweig 108 l.
Braun, Zooey, Stuttgart 187
Cook, Peter, London 208 r., 209, 211
Dechau, Wilfried, Stuttgart 152 l., 212 l., 232 l.
Denancé, Michel, Paris
    226 r. a., 227, 242 r. a., 243, 245
Deuster, Katja, Dortmund 72 l.
Dittmar, Andreas, Halberstadt 114 r. b., 115
Doiztua, Emilio P., Madrid 174–176
Double, Steve 172 l.
Duncan, Sarah 168 r.
Esch, Hans Georg, Hennef-Stadt Blankenberg
    152 r., 153, 154, 232 r. b., 233
Evrard, Jacques 24 l.
Eydel, Katja, Berlin 116 l.
Fessy, Georges, Paris 20–22
Flak, Andrea, Hamburg 104–106
Flitner, Bettina, Cologne 96 l.
Frahm, Klaus, Hamburg
    74, 75, 77, 124, 125, 127
Gahl, Christian, Berlin 121, 123
GATERMANN + SCHOSSIG, Cologne
    96 r. a.
Gavazzeni, Carlo, Milan 194 l., 228 l.
Gedda, Hans, Stockholm 190 l.
Goldberg, Stefano, Genoa 226 l., 242 l.
Graubner, Klaus, Frankfurt 128 r., 129, 131
Green, Tim 168 l.
Griffin, Matthew, Berlin 90 r., 91, 92
Guerra, Fernando, FG+SG, Lisbon
    198, 199, 201
Gullstrand, Mårten, Milan 90 l.
Hagen, Gerhard, Bamberg 223 r., 225
Hannappel, Werner J., Essen 48 r., 49
't Hart, Rob, Rotterdam 47 b.
Heiderich Hummert Architekten, Dortmund
    72, 73
Heissner, Oliver, Hamburg
    16 r., 17, 19, 52–54
Helin, Patrik Gunnar, Alingsås 191, 192 r. a.

Henriksen, Paul Ib 58, 234 l.
Hesse, Udo, Berlin 128 l.
van den Heuvel, Thea, Nijmegen
    216 r. b., 219
Hinrichs, Johann, Rott 30 r. a., 31, 33
hochbild.tv, Fitzen 15
House, Fred 56 r. b., 57
Hueber, Eduard, New York 100 r., 101, 103
Huthmacher, Werner, Berlin
    116 r., 117, 119, 172 r. b., 173
Ito, Toyo, & Associates, Architects, Tokyo
    112 r. a., 113 l.
Johnson, Ben 208 l.
Kada, Kilian, Graz 222 r. b.
Kaunat, Angelo, Salzburg 222 r. a., 223 l.
Kavanagh, Ros, Dublin 78, 79, 81
Kers, Pieters 158 l.
Keuzenkamp, Fas, Pijnacker 46 r. a.
Kida, Katsuhisa, Tokyo 182–184
Kiefer, Aloys, Hamburg 38, 39, 41
KME-TECU, Osnabrück 167
Leiska, Heiner, Hamburg 212 r., 213, 215
Lindman, Åke E:son, Bromma 190 r., 192 l.
Lippsmeier, Peter, Bochum 48
Lombardi Vallauri, Saverio, Segrate 194 r. a.
m2r Architekten, Berlin 42, 43, 45
Maggi, Moreno, Rome 194 l., 228 l.
Malhão, Daniel, Lisbon 166 r. b.
Marburg, Johannes, Geneva 26, 27, 29
Marcato, Maurizio, Verona 194 r. b., 195, 197
Matsumura, Yoshiharu, Osaka 178–180
Meinel, Udo, Berlin 186 r., 189
Meisen, Manos, Düsseldorf 64–66
Mølvig, Thomas, Brabrand 220 r. a., 221
Moran, Michael, New York 246, 247, 249
Mørk, Adam, Copenhagen
    58 r., 59, 61, 234 r., 235, 237
Müller, Stefan, Berlin 94 r. b., 95
NOX / Lars Spuybroek, Rotterdam
    202, 203, 205
Ortmeyer, Klemens, Braunschweig
    108 r., 109, 111
Passoth, Jens, Berlin 82 r., 83, 85
Peper, Sanne, Amsterdam 148 l.
Perlmutter, Michael 192 r. b.
Perrey, Rainer, Cologne (moderne stadt)
    96 r. b., 97, 99
Plissart, Marie-Françoise, Antwerpen
    24 r. b., 25

Prinz, Bernhard, Hamburg 16 l.
Provily, Philip 86 l.
Richters, Christian, Münster
    10, 11, 13, 30 r. b., 132, 133, 135, 148 r.,
    149, 151, 162 r. b., 163, 165
Riehle, Tomas, Cologne 51
van Rijthoven, Rien, San Francisco
    158 r., 159, 161
Rombouts, Johan 56 r. b., 157
Rose, Corinne, Berlin 94 l.
Ryan, Andy, Los Angeles 138, 139, 141
Serejo, Alberto, Århus 220 l.
de Sousa, Rui Morais, Lisbon 166 l.
Suárez, Daniel, Zamora 113 r.
Timmerman, Bill, Phoenix 136 r. b., 137
Tollerian, Dietmar, Linz 68, 69, 71
Tyler, Adrian, Madrid
    144, 145, 147, 238, 239, 241
UNStudio, Amsterdam 162 r. a.
Vinken, Frank, Essen 186 l.
Waldner, Helene, Vienna 100 l.
Wetzel & von Seht, Ingenieurbüro, Hamburg
    14 r. a.
Wowe, Cavaso Del Tomba 82 l.
Zwart & Jansma Architects, Amsterdam 47 a.

All other pictures were made available by the
architects

Cover
front side: NOX / Lars Spuybroek,
    Rotterdam
back side: Oliver Heissner, Hamburg (l.)
    Craig Auckland, Bristol (r.)